Because He Lives

Gloria Gaither

Because He Lives

Fleming H. Revell Company
Old Tappan, New Jersey

Scripture quotations not otherwise identified are based on the King James Version of the Bible (italics added by author).

Scripture quotations identified TEV are from Today's English Version of the New Testament. Copyright © American Bible Society 1966, 1971.

Scripture quotations identified LB are from The Living Bible, Copyright © 1971 by Tyndale House Publishers, Wheaton, Illinois 60187. All rights reserved.

Scripture quotations identified NEV are from The New English Bible. © The Delegates of the Oxford University Press and the Syndics of the Cambridge University Press 1961 and 1970. Reprinted by permission.

Lines from "The Spring And The Fall" by Edna St. Vincent Millay are from COLLECTED POEMS, Harper & Row. Copyright 1923, 1951 by Edna St. Vincent Millay and Norma Millay Ellis.

Excerpts from THE VELVETEEN RABBIT by Margery Williams. Reprinted by permission of Doubleday & Company, Inc.

Excerpts from *Knowing God* by J. I. Packer, © 1973 by J. I. Packer, are used by permission of InterVarsity Press. Published outside the United States by Hodder & Stoughton Ltd.

Library of Congress Cataloging in Publication Data

Gaither, Gloria.
　　Because He lives.

　　　1. Gaither, Gloria.　2. Gospel musicians—United States—Biography.　3. Christian biography—United States.　I. Title.
ML420.G13A3　　248　　77–10336
ISBN 0–8007–0881–4

... I have set before you life and death ...
therefore choose *life*, that both
thou and thy seed may live.

Deuteronomy 30:19

Contents

Preface

This is a personal chronicle—I don't apologize for that. If the old saying that "necessity is the mother of invention" is true in the world of mechanical innovations, then it is more true in the world of ideas. Artists—painters, writers, musicians—are driven to produce in order to make a statement, fill a void. To create is as necessary to the artist as oxygen is to the man gasping for air. And there have been times when I have felt that I would literally "choke to death" if I could not lay my hands on a sheet of paper on which to pour out the longings, inspiration, pain, or joy of my heart.

This "passion to produce" is familiar to all who have ever been driven to create, whether that creativity finds expression in what we call the fine arts—painting, sculpture, drama, writing, or music—or in the more practical arts of which daily life is made. But whatever form of expression *creativity* takes, I don't believe any of us produce much of value if we are not moved, stirred, challenged, or driven.

This brings me to the reason for this book. *It is to share the thoughts that have been the driving passion behind the songs that Bill and I have written,* the vital statement which LIFE has made to us. At the risk of sounding narrow and restricted in my thinking, I would be less than honest if I did not tell you from the onset that *we do not believe these principles of LIFE to be optional.* If we had felt they were merely another alternative to the many prevalent philosophies of life already saturating our cluttered world of thought, we would not have been so driven to spend our lives sharing them and writing songs about them. We do not believe these principles to be a "way of life," but rather LIFE itself; not a philosophy to be endorsed, but a FORCE that can move into and engulf every area of one's life.

We are not trying to organize a new school of thought or create a new discipline of study, because this LIFE of which I speak is not our invention, but the plan of the One who brought this LIFE to us. We did not invent it; we—like many others—have only made a wonderful discovery of it. Because of this, you will find that this book is not a biography of two songwriters. How pointless it would be to tell you birth dates and the human history of two people who merely discovered the wonderful life of Someone else. It will instead be a chronicle of discovery—and as such will contain perhaps some personal experiences about how this exciting LIFE came to possess us, and drove us to tell its story in song.

In telling our story we hope that if there is a restless longing for meaning in your life, it will be stilled by a personal encounter with Him who is both the cause and the satisfaction of that longing. And if your experience already affirms what we here share, we hope that you will be inspired to pursue with greater vigor and singleness of mind that joy that has begun in you.

One last thing—although I am putting the words on these pages, this book is actually from both Bill and me. Like our songs, this book is a result not only of our personal discoveries of *life in Jesus Christ* but of our life and thought together. Many of the examples and stories are my own, since I know them best, but the heart of it all is shared between us—and now with you.

Acknowledgments

A special "thank you" to my mother and to Deanie and Annie, who so often tackled the chores I had left undone to write this book; to our children, who gave me patient support and unlimited words of wisdom; and to Bill, who shared all the pain and excitement and never once retreated when trapped into listening to each new installment; and to Jan Rist, who deciphered the hieroglyphics of my longhand-in-pencil and transcribed all this into typing someone could read.

Thanks, too, to Ron and Darlene Garner for permission to include their story; to *Moody Monthly* for permission to use formerly published material ("My Most Memorable Christmas"); and to Paragon Associates and Gaither Music Company for permission to plagiarize myself and Bill from *His Love . . . Reaching,* and the many song lyrics here included.

I

Because He Lives . . .

*there is a way out of our
despair, cynicism, and
depression—to childlike trust,
hope, and joy. There is a cure.*

Answering Questions
Nobody's Asking

You'd have to be dead not to know that this world is sick —"bad sick"! Not just with cancer and heart disease and muscular dystrophy and multiple sclerosis and cerebral palsy, and various kinds of flu, but also sick with venereal disease, cirrhosis of the liver, overdoses, drug addiction, alcoholism, hypertension, emotional disorders, and nervous breakdowns. And that's just the tip of the iceberg— the part that shows above the surface. That list doesn't even begin to take into consideration all the real illnesses that may cause less obvious symptoms. I mean the kind of pain and hurt nobody sees—the kind of suffering that hides behind nice faces and expensive business suits and well-dressed children and crystal cocktail glasses. The sort of pain that rides in executive jets and sits behind corporate desks and goes to P.T.A. and enrolls in finishing schools and military academies. The list fails to count the hurts of those who live in tenement houses, wear black faces, wait for welfare checks, carry rat-infected babies to faceless clinics, or hide in stench-filled alleyways. *I mean this world is sick!*

There is good news! A cure's been found! It has been bought in limitless supply. It has been proven effective without exception. And it's free to all.

And now the bad news! Its availability is one of the best-kept secrets in history. Oh, there have been those who have leaked the information to the press, and there is a very detailed manual available, but since the cure seems "too good to be true," the news has often been ignored by those who most need it—the suspicious, the cynical, the weak, those who hurt too badly to concentrate, those who stumble on big words. And to make it worse, many of those who have tried the cure—and found it effective for themselves—have been satisfied to enjoy their health and in some cases have even felt pride and a sense of status in possessing the cure. These have harbored the secret and boxed it in, and labeled it "ours." Sometimes some who have found the cure have banded together in little groups. They have broken down the cure into parts and have chosen certain of the ingredients and claimed ownership (or at least exclusive distributorship) of those ingredients. They have in some cases become so obsessed with a particular chosen ingredient that they have named their group after it, created literature about its characteristics, and organized offices and elected officials to disseminate the information, being careful to include denials in all literature that the ingredient is even present in anyone else's supply of the "cure" and is, in fact, a test as to whether or not the cure is "real."

These various groups with their combined volumes of materials on various ingredients of their choice (none of which is effective, of course, except as a part of the *whole cure*) seem to confuse the sick. In desperation, because of their intense pain and agony, many have tried one celebrated ingredient or another, but have been so discouraged and disheartened by the disappointing result of the incomplete cure that they have given up all hope of finding help. Indeed, many have plunged themselves deeper into their skepticism and cynicism, swearing never to trust another promise of hope.

Meanwhile, the "ingredient groups" who have—don't forget—really experienced the cure for themselves and felt its marvelous effect, call meetings to discuss the decline in outside interest. They feel so comfortable in their fellowship that they mistake the coziness for the cure and merely enlarging the fellowship becomes their driving goal. How to do it? Print more materials. Invent elaborate structures of worshiping the ingredient. Bring in more exciting projects—have more contests—give bigger prizes. Print the ingredient's name and related slogans on signs and leaflets and bumper stickers. Widen the scope. Divide into age groups. Have parties and projects and attractions. Prove to the whole world that this is undoubtedly the place to get this ingredient! Be aggressive. Let them know. Gear up the subgroups. Set goals for the dissemination of literature and the raising of money to make more literature. Call delegates of each subgroup to report to a central gathering four times a year. Set quotas. Assign territory. If the sick won't respond, shake the dust from your feet and go on to those who have had the cure, but are endorsing another ingredient. Convince them that *their* ingredient is not enough. They need the new dimension of *your* ingredient. Build bigger buildings. Attract their attention. Have the best facilities in town. . . .

Absurd? Not at all. The world *is* sick. There *is* a cure. It has been bought in limitless supply. It has been proven effective without exception to all who have accepted the application and have let it be injected into the very blood of their lives. *And it is free.* But, oh, how wonderful it would be if all "religious" efforts were really an inoculation program, not caring where the application was received, but caring very much that the sick are made whole.

But the games we play and the walls and cages we build —the façades we put up and the highly complicated theological systems we devise—very effectively keep that cure from the ones who need it the most—the dying.

I am convinced that the reason the world does not take us seriously when we say we have a cure is that *we* are not serious. Too long ago we got out of touch with the life-changing applications to our own lives. We got too busy enjoying our health, reveling in our freedom, enjoying our release. We were more comfortable with other "well folks" and really didn't want to get dirty with the death and the pain by deliberately choosing to return to the world.

Accepting the cure is one thing. Accepting the Lordship of Jesus Christ is quite another. It is a gutsy risk. For those who were really serious about "cure sharing," Jesus Himself prayed:

> Keep them in the world, but not of it. Cured, but among the sick—immune as they walk with the dying —giving to them LIFE!

I want to spend my life
Giving folks the Living Water
And the Bread of Life
   They
      Just
         Can't
            Live
               Without!

Don't want to spend my time
Writing songs to answer questions
That nobody's even asking anyhow.
When the house is burning to the ground,
There's just no time to stand around,
Arranging all the pictures on the wall.

I want to spend my life
Giving folks the Living Water

And the Bread of Life
They just can't live without—
'Stead of spending all that time
Writing songs to answer questions that
    nobody's even asking, anyhow.

Don't want to spend my time
Preaching sermons that give answers
To the questions no one's asking anywhere.
When there's so much pain and hurting,
There's no time to be searching
For the needles in the haystack that aren't there.

I want to spend my time
Wearing myself out for Jesus
With the news a cure's been found
To heal our land—
'Stead of making lists, inventing creeds,
That aren't concerned with people needs,
I'll show them how to touch the nail-scarred hand.

His Love . . . Reaching

Both Bill and I used to be English teachers, and we
loved it. Maybe there's a warm spot in our hearts for
teaching because it was during the noon hour and after-
school times that we first met and shared our passion for
literature, politics, philosophy, and life. It seemed there
was so much to discover in each other that we soon decided to spend the rest of our lives at it.

But the real reason we loved teaching was a deep respect and affection for the thinking capabilities of young

people. Despite their immaturity, they are, in general, more honest and open than adults and less likely to harbor bigotry, prejudice, and pessimism. Because of this, they are very capable of deep, abstract thought and rational deductions. They are still able to dream, to hope, to believe.

The other dimension of teaching that brought us joy was the intriguing business of dealing in words, for language is the symbol of life. We have watched our own children as they have grown from babyhood to the moment they began to notice letters and then words. It is a thrill greater than their first step, when children first discover that letters are their own secret servants, that they themselves can take the puzzle pieces of an alphabet, create words that stand for the thoughts in their heads— unique to them alone—and can, by mastering and manipulating those pieces, those tools, take the thoughts from their minds and put them in the minds of another. What self-discovery! What a feeling of mastery! What a thrill of control! What freedom! To have had thoughts and feelings—joy, love, pain, anger, excitement, anticipation, invention, disappointment, music, poetry—all caged up inside a human soul . . . then to discover that one has the key that can release them all! To know that one can take into his own mind the thoughts and feelings of another, and that this sharing is neither restricted by time or space nor limited by death or distance!

Last night I watched our little son as he carefully formed the sounds of the letters with his mouth: *"Fa—fa —ee—ee—ta—ta—fffeeett—feet"!* I watched his eyes glisten and his little hands clap spontaneously as he carefully uttered a familiar word. He had heard the word all his life, but had never *seen* it. Word after word, he sounded them out, his excitement mounting with each new pronouncement. It was as if he were just now coming face-to-face with an old friend he had previously known only through telephone conversations. The words—familiar, common symbols of things in his world—were now making sense to him. The mysterious hieroglyphics of books were becoming his own secret code. There was affection in his voice as he rolled the words deliciously around in his mouth: *hand, feet, eye, sister, mother, six, daddy, hop, run, sit, puppy, cup.* His words, his secret code, his symbols! The puzzle of life coming from his own pencil. The puzzle of life for him to read at will. Words, the symbols of life.

Because of the mystery, the joy, the magic of words, and the gratitude we feel for being freed by them to share the deepest recesses of our hearts, we have enjoyed teaching the rules of the word game of language to children. We have even been privileged to be there when some began to master the skills and really started to create on their own.

Authorities say that in order to teach effectively, teachers must first convince the student that what they want him to learn is vital in some way to his life. What could be more necessary to life than words? Without them and their skillful use, we would all be autistic children, caged alone in the prison of our own minds in a universe apart from all others. Of course language is important! Of course it's necessary to our existence!

It must have been the "English teacher" in me that first drew me to an intriguing verse from the Bible: "In the beginning was the Word . . ." (John 1:1).

It was the capital *W* that captured my attention. If a word is a symbol for a thought, then this *Word* was special. It was *the* Word, the symbol of the first original thought, the one *in the beginning.* It was the idea that preceded all other ideas. It was the thought that came before any other thought. If I missed *this* thought, I would miss the basis for *all* thought, the reason behind *all* reason, the excuse for the utterance of any subsequent words!

Trembling with the excitement of discovery, I read on: ". . . and the Word was with God. . . ." Then the thought, the idea was with God, too. It was *His* idea; it was God's concept.

". . . and the Word *was* God." The Word was God! The Word and God were so much a part of each other that the Word was God and God was the Word.

My mind raced on! A Bible verse I had learned as a child came to me, a very similar line that had to do with what God is: "God is Love."

If God is Love, then love, too, had always been there with God. *Love*—God's giant, perfect, healing, total love. How I wished for a word to express it in our language! The kind of Love that God *is!* How to say it? I had felt it! I had known the power of it!

I read on: "The same was in the beginning with God. All things were made by him; and without him was not any thing made that was made. In him was life; and the life was the light of men" (vv. 2–4).

Then His Word was a creative thing. It had such power that it caused things to come alive with His life. I knew a little of what that meant. Each of us has at some time been possessed by an idea that had to find expression. At these times we know a little of the power of creativity— call it "inspiration" or "insight"—the positive passion that possesses us and drives us to express that idea in tangible form, be it music or art, cooking or sewing, tool design or building plans, invention or organization. Anyone who has ever felt it knows that he has, for a moment at least, plugged into the power of the universe—something bigger than mere human energy. It transcends the pull of aching muscles, tired eyes, loss of sleep. It drives one on and on until the work is finished, the statement is made, the inspiration is poured out, drained out into the receptacle. It is the receptacle we call the "work of art."

Then God must have planned to share a bit of the creative energy of the universe with us. It is (we don't really have a word) LOVE. It has been misused and distorted and prostituted, but all creative energy must come from God the Source. In its purest form it must have been the power that caused the universe to take form and shape. It caused things to become *alive with His life.* It was—GOD!

". . . and the life was the light of men." No wonder people down through the ages have tried to explain inspiration as "seeing a light"! The very words *insight* and *revelation* have hinted at the ability to see into things which other people miss. It must be that there are moments, fleeting moments, when God lets us mortals use His eyes. "And the life was the light of men"!

> In the beginning, God created the heaven and the earth. And the earth was without form, and void; and darkness was upon the face of the deep. . . .
>
> Genesis 1:1, 2

At first, God who is Love reached out in Creation, and His reaching had such enormous power that the firmament burst forth from His fingertips. . . . And the sun and the moon took their places. . . . And God spangled the night with a thousand stars. The waters found their way to their own boundaries and the tides were forever set. Fish and creatures of the deep found their paths in the sea.

And God went on reaching. . . .

And dry land appeared—buds burst forth. Then came fields and grasses, hills and plains. Heartbeats of animals and all living creatures throbbed at the touch of God's reaching. Even yet, Love, longing for someone to whom to give Himself, was not satisfied. For Love needs someone to receive. So God reached further—and made a man.

At first, man enjoyed in childlike wonder the companionship of his Creator and all the things that had freely been given for his use. But gradually greed obscured his gratitude and made a careless consumer of him. He began to take for granted the marvelous order and beauty that surrounded him. He didn't see that all the things which Love had created were a result of God's reaching out to him. Instead of returning God's love in thankfulness by treasuring nature's resources, man selfishly used and wasted and prostituted Creation, blindly failing to recognize that it was all intended to be the lovely backdrop for Abundant Life.

Still Love went on reaching. . . .

It was the love of Christ reaching out that caused Him to put a special value on the human person, that caused God to make man only a little lower than the angels, that gave man the treasure of being able to think and reason, to question and learn. It was God's reaching love that gave man the ability to return affection and love—to laugh and cry, to weep and rejoice.

But man misused this gift, distorted and wasted his thinking, perverted his emotions, violated his sensitivities to the feelings of others, and even used his mind to formulate theories arguing that he himself was the god of the universe and that his own mind had invented all things.

Still Love went on reaching. . . .

It was God's reaching in love that built safeguards into the universe so that man would not destroy himself. They were simple, timeless guidelines for freedom and joy. But man called them bondage, fetters, chains. He simply did not understand that the law was Love's safe harbor for his protection from the storms of himself.

Right from the beginning, Love has *reached,* and from the beginning man has refused to understand. But God's love went on reaching, risking rejection, offering itself.

Love offered the eternal—we wanted the immediate.
Love offered deep joy—we wanted thrills. Love offered
freedom—we wanted license. Love offered communion
with God Himself—we wanted to worship at the shrine of
our own minds. Love offered peace—we wanted approval
for our wars.

Even yet, Love went on reaching. . . .

> He was in the world, and the world was made by him
> and the world knew him not. He came unto his own,
> and his own received him not. But as many as received
> him, to them gave he power to *become the sons of*
> *God. . . .*
>
>   John 1:10–12

Love has always been there in the chaos of our world.
It was the Word that echoed through the formless void;
And whether in the universe or worlds of our own minds—
It is God's Love that turns that chaos into joy!

The Word that formed creation man just could not
understand;
Its sounds were muffled by his wars and strife.
And man destroyed resources God intended just to be
The lovely backdrop for Abundant Life!

And so that great Creator who'd been reaching all along,
This God who'd formed the world with His own hands—
Made Love become a baby, one of our very own,
And spoke His Word so we could understand!

So Love went on reaching
And Love went on longing
Right past the shackles of my mind—
And the Word of the Father
Became Mary's little Son—

And His Love reached all the way—
TO
  WHERE
    I
      WAS.

Worthy the Lamb

I saw him at the greeting-card rack in the drugstore. He was kind of a big awkward-looking guy with work-worn hands, and he was fumbling through the section marked BIRTHDAY—WIFE. I watched him as he picked out one or two cards, read them, put them back. I could tell by the look on his face that he wasn't finding what he wanted at all. He read a couple more and put them back. Then, looking kind of embarrassed, he picked out another. It was sort of a corny-looking card with flowers on the front —probably read something like "Roses are red, violets are blue. . . ." But he finally took it to the checkout counter and paid for it. The lady put it in a little brown paper sack, and he walked out the door.

I suppose he took it home and scrawled something simple on the bottom of it like "Love, Pete," and he gave it to her. But it really didn't say what he wanted it to say. Because, you know, it isn't easy to say the things that really matter, is it?

It isn't easy to say, *"I really love you."*

Sometimes it's hard to say, *"I acted like a child yesterday. Please forgive me."*

It isn't very easy to say, *"I'm sorry; I was wrong."*

It's hard to find the words that say, *"You're the glue that holds my whole world together, and I think sometimes if it weren't for you, I'd just fall apart!"*

You see, the things that really matter—the things we want to say—just aren't easy to say, are they?

You know, I think God tried all down through history to tell us what He really wanted us to know. Yes, I know all those words like

omnipotent
    and omnipresent
        and omniscient
            and that "nothing is impossible with God."
But people are not
omnipotent
    and omnipresent
        and omniscient.
People are
human
    and preoccupied
        and sometimes dull and scared
            and deaf to things eternal.

And God is not pushy. He is gentle and patient and persevering. So He surrounded man with the grandeur of His Creation. And He built around man the forests and trees and intricate system of the universe and the loveliness of seasons and textures and sounds and smells and tastes. And God whispered through it all: "Talk to Me. Listen to Me."

Then God gave the law, the lovely, simple system for fellowship with the universe—God's handbook of communion with all life.

But man thought the law was pushing him, restricting his "freedom." So he pushed back, he rebelled.

Then God sent His prophets and His teachers to help explain the law. They tried to tell man that if he would obey, he would be free. They said that it was man's "pushing back" that forged his chains. They said he was building his own prisons, choosing his own cages. They said that obedience was the way out of his dilemma. But man didn't want to be told. He stoned the prophets. He stamped them out of his world, then stood back, brushed his hands together, and said, "There! that should take care of those unpleasant men!"

Man had only heard part of the message. He had heard the part about God's justice, the part about how God is a Holy God and man is not very holy. He understood that when man does evil things, he somehow has to pay.

But the part God really wanted him to know—the part that says, "I Really Love You!"—

Man wasn't getting that, was he?

So God had a plan.

God must have said, "I know what I'll do! I'll send MY LOVE right down there where they are, where they can touch it and feel it and watch it grow. And I'll send it as a little, tiny vulnerable baby, so they'll *have to* touch it— and they'll have to hold it close. MY LOVE—right where they are!"

And the Bible says:

> And the Word was made flesh, and dwelt among us, [*God's love became a baby—one of our very own!*] (and we beheld his glory, [*Yes, we held in our arms and looked into the face of the specialness of God Himself!*] the glory as of the only begotten of the Father,) full of grace and truth. [*God's love that doesn't have to be deserved and all the secrets of the universe wrapped in a baby blanket in our arms!*]
>
> John 1:14

Can you feel the electricity in the atmosphere of the universe as it dawns on man for the first time: So *this* is what He meant! Can you hear for one moment the cries of the shackled from the onset of time? Can you feel the

pain of the heavy chains and fetters on the ankles and
wrists of every prisoner in every dungeon in history? Can
you feel the sting of the whip—the thud of the fist felt by
every slave who has ever taken a beating? Can you feel
the guilt and inner pain of every man who ever cheated
on his wife, every wife who ever cheated on her husband,
every parent who ever abused a child, every child who
ever betrayed the trust of a parent, every liar, every thief,
every deceiver, every murderer, every character assas-
sin? Can you feel the hot tears of grief at every graveside?
Can you feel the corporate agony of every war? Can you
know all the pain ever brought to mankind from the refusal to accept, from rebellion against the law?

Then perhaps you can begin to know the upheaval of
the sigh of relief that came to the world that day. Here is
the account by John, who was given a special insight into
the grand scope of it all:

> And I saw in the right hand of him that sat on the
> throne a book written within and on the backside,
> sealed with seven seals.
>
> And I saw a strong angel proclaiming with a loud
> voice, *Who is worthy to open the book, and to loose the
> seals thereof?*
>
> And no man in heaven, nor in earth, neither under
> the earth, was able to open the book, neither to look
> thereon. [*So here's the solution, but NO ONE could
> read the words.*]
>
> And I wept much, because no man was found wor-
> thy to open and to read the book, neither to look
> thereon.
>
> And one of the elders saith unto me, *Weep not: be-
> hold, the Lion of the tribe of Juda, the Root of David,
> hath prevailed to open the book, and to loose the seven
> seals thereof.*
>
> And I beheld, and, lo, in the midst of the throne and

of the four beasts, and in the midst of the elders, stood a Lamb. . . .

And he came and took the book out of the right hand of him that sat upon the throne. . . .

[There were angels] Saying with a loud voice, *Worthy is the Lamb that was slain to receive power, and riches, and wisdom, and strength, and honour, and glory, and BLESSING.*

And every creature which is in heaven, and on the earth, and under the earth, and such as are in the sea, and all that are in them, heard I saying,

Blessing,

    and honour,

        and glory,

            and power,

be unto him that sitteth upon the throne, and unto the Lamb for ever and ever.

Revelation 5:1–7, 12, 13

You see, a man couldn't do it—he didn't know the words. An angel couldn't do it—he couldn't speak the language. Laws didn't do it—they were only symbols, guidelines, to point the way. God had to do it—for He *was* the Word—and the Word was Love.

Oh, He's worthy, all right! Worthy of our praise, honor, blessing, and glory. He didn't give up! He wouldn't take *no* for an answer. He came all the way—to where we were—to where we are!

He could open the Book of Life. *He* could break the seals and the chains. *He* could dry the tears, still the cries, heal the wounds, ease the pain, bridge the gaps, fill the longings, neutralize the guilt. *He* knew the combination to the secret of the universe.

He knew the words. He *was* the Word.

Hear the cries of the shackled from the onset of time—
For the chains of defeat there's no key.
See the tears of the broken, the cries of the slaves:
"Is there no one worthy to set us free?"

Then the crying is stilled as the chorus rings out,
The shackled released from their chains;
And thousands of voices are swelling the song.
"Worthy the Lamb that was slain!"

Then all the archangels, the saints of all time,
Holding their crowns in their hands,
Fall down before Him, joining the song,
"Worthy, worthy the Lamb!"

Worthy! Worthy! Worthy the Lamb that was slain.

It Is Finished—The War

This chapter is about the War. It's about the longest and
most comprehensive and most hellish war in history. It
has outlasted every other war and is, in fact, the cause of
every other war. Every hatred, every act of greed, every
lust for the rights of another, every envy, and every mur-
der can be traced to this War.

Adam and Eve knew about this War as they reached in
disobedience for the fruit and saw that they were naked.

Cain knew about this War as he bludgeoned his brother
to death.

Noah knew about this War as his voice grew hoarse
from crying unheeded warnings to neighbors while he
hammered away on what was probably called Noah's
Folly.

Lot knew about the War when he felt the hand he was holding turn cold and hard as a chunk of salt as he fled up the mountain from Sodom.

Esau knew about it as his growling stomach drowned out his better judgment and he traded away his birthright for a bowl of soup.

Joseph's brothers knew about the War as they watched Joseph disappear with the Egyptian caravan before they smeared his coat with phony blood.

Pharaoh knew about it as he watched from his palace window, unmoved as his soldiers threw terrified babies into the Nile River.

Aaron knew about the War, as he molded a god he could handle and led the heathen dance at its feet.

Samson knew about the War as he snuggled his head on Delilah's shoulder and mumbled God's secrets in her ear.

Saul knew about the War as he told his lie to the music of bleating sheep and lowing oxen.

David knew about the War from his rooftop as he gazed with lust at Bathsheba bathing in the morning sun.

Jonah knew about the War as he nestled down for the night in some secret, hidden corner of a ship.

Nebuchadnezzar was aware of this War when, through bleary, drunken eyes, he saw a detached hand writing on his wall.

From the beginning of time, the War has gone on—the battle between God's infinite, unlimited love and the pull of evil—with man always caught in the middle—pulled by right, by love, by the highest in his nature, by his dreams and his hopes, yet pulled, too, by evil, greed, selfishness, and all that is base in his nature. If God had let go, man would have been abandoned to his less-than-animal self— used up, burned out, dead in the worst way. But there was also something "worth it" in man. *And God kept on loving.* The perfectness of God's love could not mix with the degenerate baseness of Satan's evil. Yet the pull of God's image in man gave man an innate knowing that there was a higher way, and he always had a longing for it. Always wanting, never having; always hoping, never achieving; always reaching, never grasping.

The War went on.

Man could not be God, and God could not come to live in the same house with baseness and evil. So man's inner self was always the battleground for this War, and every man was enlisted to fight it, but always ultimately doomed to lose. I suppose the War would have gone on forever, had it not been for God's plan to stop the vicious cycle. Man could not achieve God-likeness, but God *could* become man. If God could be a man and live to resist the pull of evil, then death could not eat away at Him. If that perfect man, then, were to die by His own choice, then the "death factor" in all men would lose its power, and the War would be over.

So God came to where man was. He wasn't half-God, half-man; he was total God choosing to become man, for only a man in the fullest sense could break the cycle. The humanity that He shared with all men surely pulled at Him, making Him vulnerable to all man's temptations, for we are told He was tempted in all points just like we are, yet He never succumbed. He was buffeted by all the forces of evil, yet He stood. Down through the ages, Satan and his demons had stalked their prey and man had struggled to resist. But now Love stepped into the gap in the form of God's own Son, and took on Himself the full brunt of the conflict, hope and freedom for all men everywhere hanging suspended on the outcome of that final War.

Now think with me how it was:

There's a line that's been drawn through the ages
And on that line stands an old, rugged cross.
On that cross a battle is raging . . .
For the gain of man's soul . . .
   or its loss.

On one side march the forces of evil:
All the demons and devils of hell—
On the other, the angels of Glory—
And they meet—
   on Golgotha's Hill.

The earth shakes with the force of the conflict,
And the sun refuses to shine
For there hangs God's Son in the balance—
And then through the darkness He cries:

"IT IS FINISHED!"
The battle is over!
"IT IS FINISHED!"
There'll be no more war!
"IT IS FINISHED!"
The end of the conflict.
"IT IS FINISHED!"
And Jesus is Lord!

But [he] made himself of no reputation, and took upon him the form of a servant, and was made in the likeness of men: And being found in fashion as a man, he humbled himself, and became obedient unto death, even the death of the cross. Wherefore God also hath highly exalted him, and given him a name which is above every name: That at the name of Jesus every knee should bow, of things in heaven, and things in earth, and things under the earth; And that every tongue should confess that Jesus Christ is Lord, to the glory of God the Father.

Philippians 2:7–11

The Prisoners Come Home

Everybody knows that "war is hell." There is no other way to look at it. War means pain and injury and heartache and agony. War means fear and spoil and death. There has never been a war, no matter how just the cause, that has not left people wondering if it was really worth it—worth all the loss, all the tears, all the unanswerable questions of blame.

The most difficult wars are the ones in which the justice and merit of the cause are less than obvious. It's bad enough to send off some mother's handsome young bundle of potential to fight for a noble and necessary cause. But when the citizens aren't convinced of the urgency of the situation and of the integrity of their leaders, it is very difficult to keep up morale in a country which feels its young are dying in vain.

Down through history there have been selfish or unjust wars. The men and women who exposed and openly took a stand against the rulers who perpetrated such wars have been hailed as heroes and heretics, patriots and traitors, depending upon the wind of public opinion at the time, and in many cases, depending upon their abilities to be as persuasive as the cunning ruler who distorted the cause.

Of all the wars of all time, the longest and most painful has been the one waged within the confines of the human soul. The battles won, the battles lost, the guilt, the self-hatred, the accusations, the gradual mortification and rotting away of self-esteem and purpose, the injury, the pain, the tears, amputations, the scars—all these horrors of any war are most terrible on the battlefields of our hearts.

In the days before the coming of Jesus Christ to our world, the War was really worth it. Although it could never be completed, it was necessary to keep fighting, lest the battles be lost and evils take over. The effort, the sacrifice, the trying to obey the law, the good works, the strict teaching, and the rigidity of worship practices were absolutely worth it. Man was fighting a foe that never gave up, and by obeying the law, offering sacrifices, trying to be a godly person, man had to live in hope that his struggle would somehow be rewarded by the mercy of God. But as for life here, the battle went on, and men had hope of salvation only through their constant struggles to obey the law and to look forward in faith to the coming of a redeemer.

But since Jesus won the victory over death and hell and evil for us forever, Satan has no more power except for one thing: *his ability to convince us that the battle has never been won.* The only power he has is the power that is given to him by those who believe his lie. Once a man is clued in to the fact that, since Calvary, Satan is power-less, and that the "blood of Jesus Christ cleanses us from all sin," he is free indeed from the ancient conflict.

One tricky little way Satan has of obscuring the victory is to make us feel that we are not worthy of the love and forgiveness of God, which is, of course, partly true. (Satan usually deals in half-truths because they are so much harder to recognize as lies.) None of us is really worthy. That was the condition of all men before Jesus came. But, you see, it is Jesus who is worthy, and He took our place as a man, lived His life in our place, and died in our place. He is our Big Brother who takes our side and fights our neighborhood battles for us. *He* is worthy, and we are *His*.

Another ploy that Satan likes to use to keep us from recognizing his defeat is to tell us to celebrate our human-ness, and since we are human, to do the things that come naturally to us as human beings and not feel guilty about them—we should accept ourselves as we are and accept others as they are and celebrate the things of this life. This, too, is a half-truth. But it is not our humanness that we celebrate. It is the Abundant Life which Jesus brought to our humanity by His death and Resurrection. This is LIFE in its real and perfect sense for us here and now while we are still on this earth. Our celebration and acceptance is of ourself as a person worthy of God's redemption because of Jesus, and of our fellowman as worthy, too, because the same love has been made available to them. We celebrate what our eyes have come to see, what our hands can feel, what our ears can hear—since He has opened our consciousness to the miracle of His life in our world.

Whenever we feel dissatisfied with life as a mere, base human, we should give thanks. That is the Holy Spirit drawing us to our New Life in Him. Without such dissatisfaction, we would never long to know "His better way." So let's celebrate the thirst for LIFE—*His* life.

I could go on and on with the ways Satan tries to cover up the facts of his defeat and Christ's victory. He's a desperate person. He must talk his way into a heart, since he has no real power except it be given by the person he convinces. But we know, don't we! And we must tell. War is hell. And purposeless war is the most hellish war of all. We see it all around: the struggle, the conflict, the walking death—so needless!

We who know must tell. We must expose the lie. We must reveal the trickery. We must publish the victory and shout out freedom. To have been loved frees us to love. To have been liberated compels us to loose the bonds that hold other prisoners captive. To have been healed of deep wounds drives us to nurse others back to wholeness.

Sometime back at the close of the Vietnam War there was a story on the evening news. It was about the same time that the prisoners of war were coming home. Do you remember how their families waited for each face to appear in the frame of the plane doorway before running to throw their arms around the one they had feared was dead? But this news story was not about a prisoner from Vietnam. This was about a soldier who had been on an island in the Pacific, and he had been there since World War II. He had been fighting there all alone, convinced that the war was still on. Oh, he'd heard rumors, but he refused to believe them until someone went to that island with proof and convinced that poor man that the war had been won thirty years before. They brought him back that day in the tattered shreds of his World War II uniform, tired, sick, emaciated—because he'd been fighting a lonely war that had already been won.

I've been there, haven't *you?* The struggle, the conflict, the hurt, the failure, the guilt—fighting the War that has already been won. We can give it up. We can claim His peace. We can feel LIFE flood in and heal up the blood-soaked battleground. We can feel the worthiness of His love put a new value on us. We can quit the struggle! We can breathe in freedom.

> Yet in my heart, the battle was raging.
> *—Not all prisoners of war have come home—*
> There were battlefields of my own making;
> I didn't know that the war had been won.
>
> Then I heard that the King of the Ages
> Had fought all the battle for me,
> And that Victory was mine for the claiming,
> And now, praise His name! I am Free!
>
> "IT IS FINISHED!"
> The battle is over!
> "IT IS FINISHED,"
> There'll be no more war!
> "IT IS FINISHED,"

The end of the conflict.
"IT IS FINISHED,"
And Jesus is Lord!

Let's tell it! Tell it to the derelict in the gutter, clasping his brown bottle: IT IS FINISHED! Tell it to the young drug addict, chained to his fix: IT IS FINISHED!

Tell it to the housewife in suburbia, hiding behind the drawn shades of her lovely home, sipping cocktails to fill the emptiness in her life: IT IS FINISHED!

Tell it to the businessman cutting corners to get ahead: IT IS FINISHED!

Tell it to the salesman hiding behind a phony smile he calls P.R.: IT IS FINISHED!

Let's tell it to the kids shuffling down the halls of our high schools, disillusioned and leaden-eyed: IT IS FINISHED!

Tell our young men and women whose dreams are slowly dying from an overdose of cynicism: IT IS FINISHED!

Tell it to the children—yours and ours—before they are tricked into the cycle of defeat and depression: IT IS FINISHED!

Tell your neighbors over the backyard fence. Stop them and shake them if you have to, but tell them, if you love them—Mrs. Jones, Mr. Phillips, Ms. Anderson:

THE WAR IS OVER!
THE VICTORY'S BEEN WON!
YOU CAN BE FREE!

There is no condemnation now for those who live in union with Christ Jesus. For the law of the Spirit, which brings us life in union with Christ Jesus, has set me free from the law of sin and death. What the Law could not do, because human nature was weak, God did. He condemned sin in human nature by sending His own Son, who came with a nature like man's sinful nature to do away with sin. . . . For sin pays its wage—death; but God's free gift is eternal life in union with Christ Jesus our Lord.

Romans 8:1–3; 6:23 TEV

II

Because He Lives . . .

> *the cure has been brought all
> the way to where we are, and
> administered so as to bring
> healing to our every point of
> need. As wholeness returns, we
> begin to recover a sense of who
> we are because of who He is.*

He Touched Me

Up to this point I have tried to show the reasonableness of God's plan of redemption and communion. But it is going to be hard for me to explain how I came to know Him for myself. The leap of faith is different for every person, and I can no more explain to you how it came to possess my life than I can tell you how I fell in love with my husband. I can tell you about Bill. I can brag about his abilities, his sense of humor, his nice hair and good face, his talent at always beating me at tennis, his willingness to let me be a better swimmer than he, his kindness to children, and his respect for his family. But I can't tell you just how it happened (or at what moment) that I came to love him. Even what I felt when I decided to become his wife does not tell you about the way our hearts have come to intertwine. I tried one time on Valentine's Day to remember just when and how our love came to be.

Where Does Love Start?

Does love have a beginning that a meeting's measured by?
Does it happen in a moment like white lightning from the
    sky?
Can you tell me its dimensions—just this wide and just this
    high?
  When did I start to love you?

Tell me just how many dates it takes for love to really start?
And just how many kisses will turn "love" into an art?

When does the magic moment come to give away your
    heart?
  When did I start to love you?

Was the day we talked of Browning the beginning of it all?
Or the time we walked the meadow and the fields of corn
    so tall
That we felt like naughty children hiding from their
    mother's call?
  When did I start to love you?

I remember just how timidly your first new song you
    shared—
And by the way you grinned I knew that you were glad
    you'd dared,
Although my evaluation wasn't worth much, still you *cared*.
  When did I start to love you?

Was it when I went to meet you in a gown of snowy white?
Was it when we signed the license and drove off into the
    night?
Was it when I gave myself to you and felt that it was right?
  When did I start to love you?

When I feared you wouldn't love me if you knew how I'd
    been wrong,
And I spent a week in mis'ry, but you'd known it all along—
And you loved me 'cause you love me, and not because I'm
    strong!
  Was it then I came to love you?

Was it when we knew for certain 'bout the baby on the
    way?
Did it start the day you told me I looked pretty—*shaped
    that way?*
Or did something special happen as we waited that last
    day . . .
  When did I start to love you?

Did it happen when we held her in our arms for the first
 time?
Was it later when I nursed her, this creation—yours and
 mine?
And I knew compared to what we held the world's not
 worth a dime!
 When did I start to love you?

There were nights we stayed and prayed by babies, fevers
 burning hot
When we really didn't know if they would make it through
 or not—
Then we'd face the dawn's beginning, thanking God for
 what we've got—
 When did I start to love you?

Was it rushing to the clinic with a bone in Amy's throat—?
Was it nights you saw me shivering and wrapped me in
 your coat?
Was it when I cleaned your bureau drawer, and found
 you'd saved my note—
 When did I start to love you?

Was it when I saw you showing Benjy how to be a man?
How to sheath his strength in meekness, how to gently take
 a stand—
How that only strength of character can salvage this old
 land?
 When did I start to love you?

When you held me close in silence when there were no
 words for grief—
When the line of empty caskets gaped at all I called
 "belief"—
When the "amen" was so final, I had you, and dared to
 leave—
 Was it then I came to love you?

What is the stuff love's made of that can cause the world
    to glow?
Is it that you made the segments that I brought you, well
    and whole?
Was it when I came to recognize the poet in your soul?
    That I began to love you?

It's not of lace and chocolate that valentines are made.
All such things are lovely but disintegrate and fade—
But love—when once it *grows* to be—is richer far than
    jade—
    I only know—I love you!

I suppose if I had known—when I first met Bill—just what our lives together would bring, it would have scared me to death! The pain and glory, the joy and sorrow, the growth and demands, the failures and the successes, the conflict of personal struggle, and the exhilaration of "becoming" have all been far beyond my early capacity to comprehend or expect.

I only know that there was a point sometime between when we first met in the school secretary's office and when we decided to get married that I chose to involve my life with this man *forever*. It was scary, too. I had been taught that divorce was not an option and that the choice of a mate was second in importance *only* to the choice of the Lord in my life. I knew, too, that if my life was going to make any sense, I had better choose to be permanently joined to a partner who had the same Lord of his life—or I could get pulled apart from within.

I will not spend a great deal of time telling you about that "magic moment." It was a deeper decision than "a flash from the blue" or "an arrow striking my heart." It was a choice, and yet it was a magical thing, too. It was a combination of reason and gut feeling. It was knowing that all the right ingredients—spiritual commitments, similar interests, compatible temperaments, families to whom we both could adjust, similar intellectual capacities —would not necessarily guarantee romance. It was knowing that "that certain feeling" could wear thin and disappear if there were not some "heavies" to build on. It was all of this. Suffice it to say that there was a moment.

Yet the days and years since have so beautifully superseded that moment, that I would not dwell on it. We have loved and grown and become. We have produced and nurtured and enjoyed children. There has been *so much* since the initial moment of commitment that is good and rich and alive. I would rather talk about all that. . . .

The Twain Shall Become One . . .

We've grown to be one soul—two parts;
Our lives so intertwine
That when some passion stirs your heart,
I feel the quake in mine.

One might suspect (who'd never known
A love so pure and true)
That this would make one twice as sad
And split his joy in two.

But I have found our oneness makes
The joys flow manifold;
And sadness touched by angel wings
Is essence rich as gold.

Love cuts away the clouds with strokes
Adept as surgeon's knife,
And leaves the trusting heart aglow
With glorious love of life!

Just as the life and love I've come to know in my marriage to Bill had a "moment of decision," there was also
a moment when I decided to invite Jesus Christ into my
life. And, as in my marriage, it was only a small moment
compared to the whole of my life as a part of God's Family. Yet, without that moment of "birth" the beautiful life
could never have begun. So let me tell you how it happened.

It was not an irrational thing. I had learned about Jesus
and His attributes and His plan of redemption. I wanted
to be free from guilt, have purpose and direction, be
plugged in to life that would go on—life that had some
eternity in it. And there was a special moment when I
made a simple childlike beginning—a leap of faith from
where I was to where I wanted to be. There was a prayer
from my heart for forgiveness. There was a sincere invitation for God's Son to come into my life and become my
new way of looking at everything. There was a feeling of
relief—almost a feeling of emptiness—not in the sense of
being vacant, but in the sense of being emptied out, clean,
and open to be refilled. In the next moments there was—
How shall I say?—a "flood of caring" for others. I guess I
would have to call it a shower of *love.* I wanted to hug the
whole world. I began to talk to my new Master about
everyone I knew, lifting their needs and hurts and heartaches to Him, making myself available for Him to use to
help answer my own prayers. I just felt *loved* and free to
take the risk of loving.

No wonder people have such a hard time finding a
name for it! Conversion—"being saved," "being transformed," "being redeemed." I guess I'd just have to call
it finding out what it really means to be loved with *God's
love,* the creative energy of the universe, the power that
shaped the worlds from nothingness. When that power
touches a mere human person, something happens! Creation all over again! Yes, I'd been touched by LOVE!

Shackled by a heavy burden,
'Neath a load of guilt and shame;
Then the hand of Jesus touched me!
And now I am no longer the same!

Since I met this blessed Savior—
Since He cleansed and made me whole—
I will never cease to praise Him!
I'll shout it while eternities roll!

He touched me!
Oh, He touched me!
And, oh, the JOY that floods my soul!
Something happened, and now I know!
He touched me!
      And
         made
            me
               whole!

Since Jesus Passed By

This morning, as I write, I am sitting at our motel window in Norfolk, Virginia. Below me in the street is a marvelous homecoming parade! Floats of every color and description proclaim that education is SERVING TODAY—BUILDING TOMORROW! Energetic and colorful bands give enthusiastic endorsement to the statement. Children, parents, high-school students, and alumni line the streets waving to the queens and officers who wave back from each float. Now and again I catch sight of a mother or father who has spotted the one who is, for them, the most important person in the parade. I can tell by the way they wave excitedly and run along the curb, trying to keep that special son or daughter in sight as long as they can.

Just across the street a row of preschoolers in pink romper suits and tiny, furry jackets line the curb. It is just the right height to make a perfect perch to rest their tiny legs. This parade must seem like a wonderland of color and sounds to them. I catch the contagion of their excitement as they tap their little heels to the rhythms and clap their hands.

Confetti drifts in green and yellow clouds on the crisp October breezes. Mounds of golden popcorn and paper cupfuls of cider disappear, completing the total sensory experience. I love a parade!

When Bill and our little Suzanne return from the choir workshop, all that will be left will be the silent clues to this lovely moment: scattered bits of confetti, empty paper cups and popcorn boxes, petals from chrysanthemum pom-poms, a few tattered crepe-paper streamers from the floats—maybe a broken lawn chair or two. They'll probably ask me why the street is so littered, and I'll say, "Why, a parade went by this morning! I'm so sorry you weren't here."

A few years back on Palm Sunday there was a terrible tornado that ravaged central Indiana. Whole villages were practically wiped out. Trailer parks were smashed and broken. Bill and I drove along the route the tornado had taken, and everywhere we looked there were destruction and death and sadness. It was so disheartening to see the storekeepers standing outside their destroyed places of business, trying to assess the damage. One brand-new subdivision of brick homes was almost completely flattened.

But it was somehow even sadder for us to see what had happened to the countryside. Forests that had taken years and years to grow were uprooted and twisted like little twigs. Crops that someone had planted and nurtured were flooded and flattened. And those big, old, two-story Indiana farm homes that had been handed down from generation to generation—destroyed. We passed one such farmhouse. All that was left of it was the hearth. One could almost hear the voices of the children it had warmed and the families that had come in after a hard day in the fields to sit by its fire and share a warm supper meal. Now, on the rubble of what had been their home, were a man and his wife about seventy years old. She had on a print apron and he his bib overalls, and as they looked at what had been a lifetime of hard work, they wept like little children.

We passed another farmhouse. This one was all gone except for the framework. Even the furniture and appliances were blown about the yard and broken. Some friends who were with us in the car told us that the family had been killed. There had been small children and the storm had struck in the wee hours of the morning. Just before we pulled away, I noticed something that I have never quite been able to forget. Slung over a rafter atop what had been the second story was a doll that had belonged to a little girl—a gruesome reminder of what had happened at that place. As we drove on down the highway, I couldn't get that sight out of my mind, that symbol of the tragedy of it all.

Then I began to wonder what it would have been like to walk down a street where Jesus had walked. My, what a different thing that would have been. . . .

Maybe you've never met this man Jesus, never heard His name. But as you walk down the cobblestone street you can tell that something surely has happened there, for here at the side of the road is a broken crutch that someone has thrown high in the air and let bound to the pavement, never to be retrieved! You walk on a little farther and there is a pile of dirty, rotten, stinking bandages that some leper has torn away—when he looked and found his skin as clean and new as a child's. You walk on a little more and there is a mattress on which some friends had brought a paralyzed man to the scene—and he left it there, because he *walked* his way home!

You see all these things, but you don't quite understand. You see a man way down at the end of the street, so you decide to ask him what it all means. You rush up to him, intending to ask him, but there is something about him that makes you stop. Here is a grown man, holding in his hands a delicate rose. The way he's holding it—gently, almost worshipfully—that's strange enough. But when you see his face, the gaze in his eyes, the tears streaming down his cheeks, it dawns on you that this man is seeing a rose *for the very first time!* You stand still out of respect for a moment and then, when you dare, you touch him on the arm and you ask, "Mister, what happened here? What does it mean?" He looks up at you with his eyes as wide open as he can get them, and he says, "Oh, friend, weren't you here? Haven't you heard? *Jesus passed by!* Jesus passed by! You see, I was born blind. Had no hope of ever seeing, and this man they call Jesus passed by this very road, and He touched my eyes, as He touched so many others. Oh, I wish you could have been here!"

He can't stay to talk any longer and, still holding the rose in his hands, he runs down the street calling for his friends. "John! Matthew! Come look at me! Jesus passed by!" And he calls to his wife and says, "Mary, Mary, come here—and bring me the babies! Oh, Mary, I've held them on my lap, and I've touched their little faces with my hands, but I've never seen what they look like. Mary, things are going to be different. So different. Jesus passed by! Jesus passed by. . . ."

I wasn't there that day on that road, but I've been on many a "street" where Jesus has passed by, and everywhere He walks, He leaves behind a trail of wholeness and completeness and joy that are unmistakably "His touch."

I guess when it comes right down to it, that is why I believe. Theology is an interesting school of thought. The Bible is beautiful literature. Sitting in a quiet sanctuary, bathed in the amber light from stained-glass windows, having my jangled nerves soothed by the chords from an organ—all that is inspiring. But to tell you the truth, when I leave the classroom, close the back door, and walk out into the real world, it is the indisputable proof of changed lives that makes me a believer.

Therapy and counseling can help a man understand and accept what he is—but only the touch of the creative power of *love* as expressed to our world in Jesus Christ can transform permanently what a man is, dismiss his past, possess his future, and make him sing:

> Like a blind man I wandered
> So lost and alone—
> Like a beggar—so helpless—
> Without God or His Son.
> Then the Savior in mercy
> Heard and answered my cry—
> And, oh, what a difference
> Since Jesus passed by.
>
> All my yesterdays are buried
> In the deepest of the sea;
> That old load of guilt I carried
> *Is all gone!* Praise God, I'm free!
> Looking for a bright tomorrow
> Where no tears will dim the eye—

Oh! There's such a difference
Since Jesus passed by!

Since Jesus passed by,
Since Jesus passed by.
Oh! What a difference,
Since Jesus passed by!
Well, I can't explain it,
And I cannot tell you why,
But, Oh! What a difference—
Since Jesus passed by.

I'm Free

On the nation's 200th birthday the President was at Valley Forge, a spectacular fleet of tall ships was sailing through the New York Harbor past the Statue of Liberty, and people everywhere were meeting in churches to pray for salvation—their own and that of our country.

But in Alexandria, Indiana, the Gaithers held their annual Fourth of July picnic and hillside gathering. Our hillside overlooks the parking lot of the Alexandria-Monroe High School where the local Chamber of Commerce puts on our annual fireworks display. And in front of our porch the lawn chairs were lined up, and this year we grown-ups were to be treated to a special Bicentennial pre-fireworks parade. It was spectacular. There was Suzanne as Uncle Sam in a tall red-and-white construction-paper top hat—and her cousin Trina as Miss America twirling a baton. They were followed by Benjy, the Town Crier who announced the gala event, and little Becky in the crepe-paper-covered wagon as Betsy Ross, sewing fervently on the "first American flag." Next came Mitchel, carrying Daffy Duck in a decorated cage—and Amy, pushing in her doll buggy the rabbit, Oscar, with a big red-and-blue ribbon around his neck. There were two fancy tricycles and another wagon in which Sing-Kai, our friendly Lhasa apso, proudly rode.

As the procession came to a halt in front of the grandstand (or, in this case, the lawn chairs), all the little voices led us in a rousing chorus of "America the Beautiful." Then our mighty patriots passed around the ice-cold watermelon, and we all settled down to watch the sky light up with stars and rockets and color.

Oh, there may have been grander celebrations, but certainly there were none dearer. It was national freedom at the grass roots. It was liberty where it counts, and I found myself breathing a prayer for those tiny patriots of our parade—that it might ever be so.

There is something in the heart of every person that longs for freedom. It is a longing strong enough to break the strongest fetter and loose the tightest bond. The secret that freedom exists seems to have been breathed into man with the very first breath of life. Every prisoner has known it. Every slave has felt it. Somewhere, way down in the deepest recesses of our souls, we know that there is freedom.

Men have died while reaching for it. Women have been kept alive by dreaming of it. Babies are driven from the womb by the pull of it. The aged find courage to walk into the valley of the shadow of death by the promise of it.

Tyrants have tried to suffocate it, demagogues have tried to impose limits on it. Anarchists have tried to prostitute it. Libertines have eroded its promise. Dictators have tried to monopolize it and save it for the elite few.

But sooner or later, like the down of a dandelion blown by the wind, the rumor of freedom is passed along from spirit to spirit, from slave to slave, from father to child, from prisoner to prisoner. Somehow we know. We all know. Try as they may, there are no forces that can forever kill freedom. It crops up. It leaks out. It oozes through the cracks and rises on the wind. Freedom! It sings its way—a note at a time, a note here and there— it sings its way into a song:

> Free at last!
> Free at last!
> Thank God Almighty,
> I'm free at last!

We would fight for it, wouldn't we? We would tell its secret to our children at any cost. We'd risk nearly anything for freedom—for a life of bondage is no life at all. No one would choose to be a slave, to be made a fool of and degraded and walked on. No one would choose to be a prisoner, to trade the sweet summer breeze and the blue sky for the steel-gray nothingness of hour upon empty hour in a barren prison cell. We wouldn't think of letting some government take over our people and turn them into purposeless, mindless masses. We'd fight. We'd tell. We'd shout out hope! We'd shout out freedom!

And yet, at this moment new chains are being forged and locked into place on some of those nearest and dearest to us. Prisons are being built to destroy freedom. These prisons are sometimes camouflaged and difficult to see, for they are not made of mortar and stone; the cells are not of iron bars and steel locks. And strangely enough, the people who are about to settle for life without freedom are the ones who are working with the enemy to forge the very chains they will one day wear.

They do this because of the intense enemy program of propaganda that convinces the victim that the doorway to slavery will be instead the threshold of liberty. Yes, the horrible irony of it is that so many are choosing slavery because they believe they are seeking personal freedom —freedom to do their own thing. It is a program of word games in which familiar words are actually given opposite meanings. For instance: *good* means "bad," *silly,* "naive." *Evil* means "adventuresome," *daring,* "fun." *Respectful* means "cowardly," *chicken,* "soft." *High* means "unconscious, out of one's mind." *Liberal-minded* means the ability to read about, see, or try any immoral act without feelings of guilt. And *freedom* actually denotes the imprisonment of freedom.

And so people we love fall prey to the clever trick, the intricate plan to kill *freedom,* not just national freedom but *internal* freedom. It's an old trick. It's been going on for centuries. And it's serious, because if freedom can't live in the heart of man, it can't live at all. "Free nations, free countries, free cities" are only figures of speech if freedom is dead in the heart. But when freedom lives within, no law can kill it, no master can enslave it, no walls can imprison it—and death only liberates it.

> Jesus said to them, "You are truly my disciples if you live as I tell you to, and you will know the truth, and the truth will set you free."
> "But we . . . have never been slaves to any man on earth! What do you mean, 'set free'?"
> Jesus replied, "You are slaves of sin, every one of you. And slaves don't have rights, but the Son has every right there is! So if the Son sets you free, you will indeed be free—"
>
> John 8:31–36 LB

Let freedom ring!
Keep it alive in the hearts of men. Whisper the high

calling of freedom to the children. Breathe it in their ears as you tuck them in at night. Write it on the doorposts of your house. Make it the theme of your song, the substance of your dreams, the hope of your days.

Breathe in freedom! Breathe out freedom!

Tell the world that when the Son sets us free, we are free indeed.

Slaves can have it, and their masters cannot squelch it.

Rich men can have it, but their money cannot buy it.

Poor folks can have it, and their poverty will not drain it away.

Children can have it, and their living will never use it up.

Old men can have it, and inactivity will not rust it.

All may share it, but none can earn it. It is the gift of the Son.

> So long I had searched for life's meaning,
> Enslaved by the world and my greed;
> Then the door of my prison was opened by love,
> For the ransom was paid—I was freed!
>
> I'm free from the guilt that I carried,
> From the dull, empty life I'm set free;
> For when I met Jesus, He made me complete:
> He forgot the foolish man I used to be.
>
> I'm free from the fear of tomorrow!
> I'm free from the guilt of the past—
> For I've traded my shackles for a glorious song.
> I'm FREE! Praise the Lord! Free at last!

The song of the redeemed. There is no sweeter freedom song. Indeed, without it, there are no other freedom songs. Those still enslaved may not understand it, but they'll notice it. They'll hear the strange refrain and something deep inside them, some ancient, timeless longing will stir. The song will seem at once unknown and yet familiar. Because deep inside of every soul, there is a secret knowing, the haunting possibility of *freedom.* And when they ask—and they will ask—share with them the song.

Make it clear. Make it true. Sing with joy. Let the song of the redeemed, the song of *freedom,* ring!

> You ask me why my heart keeps singing,
> How I can sing when things go wrong—
> But, since I've found the Source of music,
> I JUST CAN'T HELP IT!
> God gave the Song!
>
> Come, walk with me through fields and forests.
> We'll climb the hills and still hear that Song,
> For even hills resound with music—
> They just can't help it,
> God gave the Song!
>
> Too many nights without dawn's promise,
> Too many days without a song—
> Then Jesus came and gave life meaning,
> Day after day the Song goes on;
> For since I've found the Source of music,
> I just can't help it—
> GOD GAVE THE SONG!
>   GOD GAVE THE SONG!

I Am Because ... He Is

When I was a little girl, there was nothing quite so exciting as spending the night at Grandma's house. She lived in the country and had none of the conveniences we had in town, such as running water, electric lights, and indoor plumbing. The farm was a magic place to a child, with morning-glory vines winding their way up binder-twine trails to the porch roof where bees and helicopter hummingbirds darted, softly stealing nectar. There were carnations breathing their clovelike fragrance into the breeze.

There was so much to do there. There were two cows I helped Grandpa to milk, butter to churn, vegetables and fruit and gladioli to pick, and eggs to gather into Grandma's big, full-length apron's skirt. It was a special place, too, because of the freedom that came with it. A child could do nearly anything at Grandma's farm: make mud pies, wallpaper the outhouse, mow her own initials into the grass in the backyard with the push mower, climb trees, make "ladies" out of hollyhocks, drink tea. . . .

But I guess it was the presence of Grandma herself that made it all so special—the way she touched things as only can the folks whose hands have had to compensate for nearly blinded eyes. I was not the only one to know her gentle touch: the hens and stray dogs and snapdragons knew it, too. I loved to watch those hands—the way they pushed and shoved the bread dough back and forth across the floured wooden board, the way they felt the stems of melons to see if they were ripe. She touched with love because her dimmed eyes just could not express it.

I watched her punch down the bread; then, while it rose again, I watched her coax the wood-stove oven to just the right temperature to bake the loaves to golden brown. I watched her use her wooden paddle to punch and squeeze the liquid from the butter once the lump was formed. But best of all I loved the times of picking blackberries in the woods behind the field. She'd take her wicker basket lined with Tuesday's *Enquirer and News,* and I'd skip ahead toward the thicket where the berries grew. There was an old car back there—a blue one—rusting away. It made a fine home for the pair of skunks that came there every summer to raise their young. I watched them—very respectfully—from a safe distance.

There were many times as I ran ahead of her that I would look back over my shoulder and see Grandma praying at the stump of an old tree. I would play until she had finished and caught up with me; then we would pick the basket full and go on home.

At supper, Pa would light the lamps and sometimes play his harmonica while Grandma fixed potato soup and sliced the bread, and I would set the table. When we were through, Grandma would take down the guitar and pick some lovely old hymn tune from its strings and sing:

> Blessed assurance, Jesus is mine!
> Oh, what a foretaste of glory divine!
> Heir of salvation, purchase of God,
> Born of His spirit, washed in His blood.
>
> Perfect submission, all is at rest,
> I in my Saviour am happy and blest,
> Watching and waiting, looking above,
> Filled with His goodness, lost in His love.
>
> FANNY CROSBY

There was something about the way she sang the strange words—like she owned them, like they were her own and they brought her joy. It brought joy to me, too.

When it came time for sleep, she would tuck me into a big bed, taller than I was. It was in a room that wasn't heated in the winter and on those nights I would be covered with a feather bed that seemed to get everything warm but my nose. Grandma would tiptoe out and sit with Pa in the "front room," until he went to bed. After she thought I was asleep, I would hear her old knees kneeling on the linoleum by the rocking chair, and I would hear her soft, sweet voice, praying for me—praying that God would guide and protect my little life and keep me from evil.

Hers were not the only prayers prayed for me—and for Bill. There have been other saints along our paths. There was Bill's Grandpa Grover who said very little about his inner convictions but simply and quietly lived it all out as he went about his business. We all loved him. To Bill, as a young boy growing up, he was a stabilizer and a rock. We all loved his sense of humor and the way he would stand back and grin as we young, rambunctious colts would learn lessons from our experiences. Yet he never said, "I told you so," or moralized on the lesson learned. He just quietly went on with life, accepting as permanent the maturing we had done. Only at his funeral did we really learn the scope of the Christlike things he had done for people at their time of need—for, true to his style, he never breathed a word of them himself.

There was Mom Hartwell, Bill's grandmother, who was just as verbal and anxious to share her faith as Grover had been silent. She sang about it in poems and talked about it with her neighbors. She tucked it into loaves of homemade bread and fresh canned peaches and gave it away to anyone who came to her door. For its sake she adopted any child who needed a place to stay, and fed any hungry vagrant. For love of her Lord she wore to shreds her treasured Bible and died singing in her delirium, "For He is so precious to me."

There was Ione Lloyd, the part-Indian pioneer woman preacher who'd as soon hunt and fish as preach, yet who had an uncanny sensitivity to the hurts and needs of people, even miles away. Her wisdom, her advice, and her prayers were the redemption of many a young life. She came to our home whenever she made her itinerant visits to what had grown to be her nationwide "parish." When she prayed, things happened, and we learned to be very careful what we asked her to pray about. I kept her phone number in my billfold, as one would emergency numbers, for those times when we needed the strong support of someone with a direct line to the Throne.

There were loving pastors and dedicated teachers and concerned parents. There was every personality, every style. But the important thing was what the Lordship of Christ did in a life.

As Bill and I were growing up, we watched, as most youngsters do, the lives around us, and it was the statement of the lives more than the statements of the liturgy we best remember. There are no laboratories for proving the validity of a philosophy of life—except life itself. There are no "test tubes of the Spirit," except the resulting expression in daily choices and value judgments of the people who are possessed by the Spirit.

When I was in college, struggling over the doubts and questions so common to the young, I remember going to my room one day, all mixed up and confused by trying to decide whether I had been deluded into accepting what I'd been taught or whether the words of Christ were really valid. There were so many opposing philosophies, so many logical schools of thought, so many problems in the world, so many pulls and attractions, so many contradictions. I sat on my bed alone, sorting through it all, and I came to the conclusion that the mind of man cannot reason it all out, that questions only bring on other questions in the realm of reason alone.

The nearest thing to proof was the lived-out result in the lives of those who had abandoned themselves to Jesus, simply and wholly. The counter-evidence could be found by tracing the final result of lives that had been fully committed to reason alone, or to material things alone, or to physical pleasure alone, or to social programs alone. The evidence seemed to reveal that those who risked everything to simply trust Jesus also found emotional stability, intellectual stimulation and satisfaction, physical fulfillment in simple pleasures, and a way to relate to others lovingly and helpfully.

Proof? No. Belief is a risk and always will be. But the lives in which I have seen wholeness and completeness have been, very simply, totally committed to Jesus Christ.

That day in college, I chose to reaffirm that commitment myself. I didn't have any big theories to offer anyone else. I didn't believe in "having a religion" to sort of round out my life, but I found that this matter of accepting the claims of Jesus Christ—betting everything I was and had on a "way beyond proof"—really worked. And I guess for me that's what mattered after all.

Bill had a similar experience the year after graduating from high school. He had always loved gospel music and the harmony of voices, so when a quartet called for him to join their group, he chose to go with them and forget about college. He had sung with his brother and sister but he'd always wanted to sing with a professional group. Here was his big chance. It wasn't very long before the glamour and the glory of his dream began to wear into the stark reality of bookings and food to eat and bills to pay. There were empty hours to spend trying to discover what was wrong. There were the usual internal struggles inside the group, the pointing of fingers, the accusations, the trying to find new styles, new songs, new arrangements, new methods. But all the while, the Holy Spirit was dealing with the young pianist about *why* he wanted to sing: what his motives were. Gospel music is by definition a song of "personal testimony." It demands something of the person who sings it. It is a way to share in music the deep experiences of the heart. Gradually, the claims of the Gospel began to make some serious demands on the young man who wanted to "just sing." He had been to the altar back home. He'd been "saved" at camp meeting— and revivals, youth meetings, and regular church services. But this was something more.

The young man had a feeling that if he risked making a commitment on the level of his motives and intentions and reasons for his choices, it would mean relinquishing control of his "want to's." He might even have to give up singing. Bill might have to see whether God had something else in mind for his life. Only those who love something dearly can understand the conflict in his heart during those lonely months away from home. Should he just use his abilities and go on working to become a success at what he loved—or should he risk the possibility of giving up what he loved to be God's total person, whatever that meant? To complicate the agony, the group began to get some breaks: a radio broadcast, some good bookings. Things were looking up.

But in Bill's heart he knew that, succeed or fail, he had come face-to-face with a problem that had to be resolved: the problem of the Lordship in his life. There was an engagement at a fairgrounds one night. He should have felt glad, elated, but instead the sense of purposelessness and emptiness had grown. After the fans and his companions were gone, he walked alone out onto an empty ball field. He looked up into the blackness of a sky studded with stars. The emptiness of his heart had grown into a longing more consuming than pain. "Oh, God!" he finally cried. "There has to be more than this! If You're there at all, take my life and do what You want with it." There was no answer, just a quiet knowing that tomorrow he'd pack his bags and head back home.

I wish that I could tell you that since the day of our initial commitments, since the day we struggled through those first doubts, that I have never had a doubt or struggle since. But I can't. Neither can Bill. Doubts and struggles are woven into the very fiber of our humanness. Our minds still grope to know the ultimate things of the Spirit, but our humanity veils the final clarity of all God has for us. We aren't the first to feel this frustration with our limitations.

> . . . we can see and understand only a little about God now, as if we were peering at his reflection in a poor mirror; but someday we are going to see him in his completeness, face to face. Now all that I know is hazy and blurred, but then I will see everything clearly, just as clearly as God sees into my heart right now.

> 1 Corinthians 13:12 LB

The important thing is the risk of believing, the commitment of accepting, and the opening of ourselves in receiving Christ's claims in our lives. These begin the miracle of discovery and throw wide the door to His life in us.

> I put on many faces
> And I tried out many places—
> Just looking for a place that felt like home—
> But I found no one to want me,
> It was all a foreign country,
> 'Til I found the Lord and claimed Him for my own.

Like the cool refreshing breezes
Was the love that came from Jesus;
He could heal the hurts that no one ever sees—
Where there used to be resentment,
There's a core of deep contentment—
In the middle of the storm I now have peace.

I live because . . .
I can because . . .
I am because . . .
    HE IS.

III

Because He Lives . . .

> *we find courage to face and deal
> realistically with doubts,
> conflicts, and obstacles.*

My Faith Still Holds

So often it has been called "the leap of faith." I like that. No matter how long the line of preparation and quest, one comes at last to the end of his ability and finds still yet ahead that land of "something more." Between the two points, there is always a gap. Some come sooner to the point of admitting their limit than others. Some refuse to admit it at all. Only the honest dare.

Bill and I have talked often with young doubters and we have observed that there are two kinds of seekers. There are the ones who really want and long to find answers and are willing to take the risk of reckoning with what the truth may demand of them. Then there are those we call the "professional doubters" who make a career of asking ever grander questions, fearing that if they stop to grasp the answers, life would require them to align their values and behavior accordingly. Much safer then to spend one's life in a perennial bull-session, philosophizing about the giant "unanswerable" questions, than to deal one by one with the answers each day reveals.

For example, it is much safer to talk about the Malthus Theory in relation to world hunger than to take on the kid across the street and help him learn to be a dependable yard worker, or to encourage his mother to keep working at her craft by helping her sell some of her work at an art fair. It is easier to talk about the evils of war and the need for unilateral disarmament than to forgive a neighbor and love one's mother-in-law. It is easier to discuss race relations and donate a few "love hours" a week to Urban League than it is to lovingly get involved indefinitely with a Vietnamese family, or really enjoy and nurture the friendship of a person of not only another race but another socio-cultural background. In the spiritual world, it is easier to keep asking theological questions—and puzzling over the authenticity of Noah's Ark—than to abandon oneself to the claims of Jesus Christ.

Sooner or later, however, anyone who is honestly seeking an end to the hunger and thirst that is inherent in the human soul will one day find himself at the brink—where he must either turn back or take the leap of faith. This is the point when he realizes that he can't work out the problems of life by his own efforts.

I guess the reason Jesus said so much about how easy it is for simple people like children to believe is that they admit sooner to being at the brink. But all of us, no matter how complicated the meanderings of our pilgrimage, must one day come to that childlikeness of admitting, "There is nothing in my abilities or my brain or my money or my strength or my sphere of influence that will get me from where I am to where I long to be."

It seems as though the human in us drives us to try *everything* before simply admitting that we need help. The paths we take are as ancient as Solomon's. Bill and I recently reread the Book of Ecclesiastes and found our present generation at every turn. He, too, tried it all. There truly is "nothing new under the sun" (*see* 1:9).

He begins with a very existential statement. "In my opinion, nothing is worthwhile; everything is futile," he says (Ecclesiastes 1:2 LB). Nonetheless, from there he goes on to seek a way to make his life a thing of value—to give himself an excuse for existing. (If we *really* think the whole thing is nothingness, why do we bother? The fact that we do bother is in itself a dead giveaway to the presence of a greater ground of being.)

First he tried to find his answers in education, in philosophy. He became so smart that he is still called the wisest man who ever lived. Yet filled with all knowledge and wisdom of the world, he cried, "I said to myself, 'I am better educated than any of the kings before me in Jerusalem. I have greater wisdom and knowledge.' So I worked hard to be wise instead of foolish—but now I realize that even this was like chasing the wind" (1:16, 17 LB).

Next he tried fun. Then drinking. Then folly—just doing anything that came to his head. These, too, left him empty and unfulfilled.

Next he tried great public-works programs, and he had the money to back up his creative and philanthropic imagination. He got into real-estate development that included homes, vineyards, gardens, parks, and orchards with a great irrigation system to keep it all productive. He bought slaves and acquired great herds and flocks. He got richer. This led him to a more cultured circle. He became interested in the arts. He started lovely choirs and orchestras. He denied himself nothing that brought him pleasure. But as he stood back and looked at it all, he found that it was all empty and useless in itself.

Back to learning he went. This time it was comparative philosophies, asking bigger and more profound questions —and all of his philosophical questions came up with this answer: "So now I hate life because it is all so irrational; all is foolishness, chasing the wind" (2:17 LB).

"I'll live for the moment," he said. "I'll keep it simple. I'll just enjoy a simple diet, enough to drink, my family, and my work." But this then gave him time to look around at common people and he discovered that there was crime, injustice, or corruption in high places. He saw oppression and tears and despair. He saw the way envy and greed and jealousy drove the wheel of fortune. He observed that this greed was not based on need, for even the men who had no family to support or leave their riches to

were just as grasping as those who were in need. He saw
hypocrites in religion. He heard people making rash promises to God, yet doing nothing about keeping those
promises. He saw red tape and bureaucracy. He saw
people depressed by bad investments and unwise spec-
ulations.

"All of life is empty," he said, for he'd tried it all. So
finally Solomon the Great came to the brink—the end of
what his humanity could achieve, intellectually, socially,
culturally, physically, emotionally, and spiritually. He,
too, had to become as a little child. And in the simplest
way he discovered life in its biggest sense. He summed it
up like this: "Here is my final conclusion: fear God and
obey his commandments, for this is the entire duty of
man" (12:13 LB).

It's scary, that moment of total abandonment. But
sooner or later, if we're honest in our search for the cure
of our ills and the nourishment for our hungers, we will
find ourselves at the brink. The choices are two: jump—
or turn back to the emptiness. I wanted "out" badly
enough; I jumped. My hunger and thirst drove me to it.
And once I abandoned my silly holdings, I found, not an
irrational never-never land, but a reality more reasonable
than any finite reason I had known. And that illusive stuff
called "faith," I found to be a concrete and substantial gift
from God, a treasure beyond communication, freely
given in exchange for my risking to let go. It had been
there all the time, not in me, but in Him. I had been trying
to conjure up faith in "faith." He only wanted me to let
go so He could give me faith . . . in Him.

> I thought I had to *see* and *feel*
> To prove that what I loved was really real—
> But passion turned to ashes, things I held to dust,
> I found "reality" in simple trust.

I tried to find life's mysteries,
Just by the reason of my mind to see;
But void remained 'tween me and where I longed to be—
'Til childlike faith there built a bridge for me.

And, oh, what joy to walk this way!
I follow nail-pierced footprints all the way.
And though the end of where I'm bound I may not see,
I choose to place my trust in Calvary.

Now years have passed since in my youth,
I weathered storms of doubt in search of truth—
Sweet Jesus calmed the tempest of my soul's unrest,
Praise God! The Calvary Road has stood the test!

My faith still holds on to the Christ of Calvary!
Oh, Blessed Rock of Ages, cleft for me!
I gladly place my trust in things I cannot see—
My faith still holds on to the Christ of Calvary!

I Believe—Help Thou My Unbelief

Before Benjy started to kindergarten I made up my
mind that this time I was going to take it like a champ.
We'd been through the first-day-of-school stuff twice before with the girls, and this time I wasn't going to get
emotional about it.

Benjy couldn't wait! And he was most distressed when
he learned that the girls were going to have two full days
of school before the kindergarten was to actually begin. So
we did our best to fill those days with activities to make
the time go easier. We went with him on Monday to the

school to see his room and pay his fees. On Tuesday I went back to meet his teacher, the principal, and the librarian. But these introductory moments didn't last long, so the rest of the time we spent buying tennis shoes, Elmer's Glue-All, crayons, a big box of Kleenex (Bill said, "That's for the teacher!"), and making a "kindergarten box" for keeping his supplies neatly in place on the shelf. We went to the fruit market and bought some tomatoes so we could use the sturdy box with the wire handle. We helped Benjy cover it with orange construction paper and paste animal pictures cut from *Ranger Rick* on the side. We made a painting smock. We counted out his milk money. Everything was ready—especially Benjy.

Wednesday morning the children all piled into my little blue car and we started for the school. Both the girls offered to walk Benjy to his room, since they each would use separate entrances, and he'd have to go alone. But, no, sir! He wasn't about to have any big sisters walking him to his room. He knew the way. He'd been there twice before and he knew *the way!* So when I pulled up in front of the elementary school and kissed them all good-bye, I watched that little guy swagger up the walk alone, his head held high, his orange kindergarten box under one arm, and his big box of Kleenex under the other. *This will be the beginning of a new phase in his life,* I couldn't help thinking. *He'll never be quite the same again. Help him, Lord.*

Now, I knew that little fellow. I knew that, in spite of the big brave façade on the outside, there was a very timid little person on the inside. *If he only knew,* I thought, *that kindergarten was more than just a place you go. If he knew that kindergarten was something that* happens *to you, if he knew about failing and competition and ridicule, he'd never step one foot out of this car.* But in his innocence (or ignorance) he charged right in through those front doors and disappeared from my sight

—and my jurisdiction. And I did exactly what I promised myself I wouldn't do. I cried. I cried for the innocence that would never be quite the same. I cried mostly for myself, because letting children go, even a little at a time, is not easy for a mother to do.

Well, I wasn't quite ready to go home—I knew it would be very quiet there—so I went out to Bill's mom and dad's house for a second cup of coffee. When I pulled into the driveway, Bill's dad hollered at me from atop a ladder where he was scraping paint from the woodwork of the rental house next door. "Where's the kids?" (Grandpas know *just* what to say!) I walked up to the ladder and stood there babbling on about how Benjy had not been afraid at all, how he'd walked right in alone and. . . .

He went right on scraping as if he wasn't hearing a thing I was saying until finally he said, "Had to move the water trough this morning. Thought there might be some rats under it." (I couldn't figure out what *this* had to do with anything.) But he went on: "Sure enough," he said, "when I looked down under there, there was a nest of baby rats; musta been nine or ten of 'em. And they looked up at me like they belonged there. I left the hole uncovered. I s'pose the cat will get in." Then he stopped scraping and looked down at me. "Kids are really confident when they don't know what they're getting into, aren't they?"

He'd heard me all right. And in his special way, he'd answered. I went on in the house, had my coffee, then drove back home. The house *was* quiet. I thought about and prayed for Benjy all morning as I did my work. *Let it be a good beginning for him,* I prayed. *Let him have some good moments to whet his appetite for learning.*

At noon I went to get him. They came out single file in a long line, all waving papers and wearing little cardboard hats; but with all the sameness, I didn't have any trouble at all spotting Benjy. I'd seen that walk before, that crooked little grin. I knew him right away. He was ours. He scooted into the backseat and stuffed his papers under my nose. "Look, Mom! what I made!" he shouted in my ear. "And I made some new friends, and my teacher's fine, and Mom—school's okay!"

As I pulled up in front of the bakery, I knew I had been the one who'd had the most to learn today. Benjy had been right. He *did* know the way. Maybe all we have to know is The Way.

. . . and Jesus said, "I AM THE WAY . . ."

I guess if we knew all it would entail when we sign up to follow Jesus, it would scare us to death. But Jesus said, "Don't worry about all that. Just trust Me. Learn of Me. Drink in all there is of Me. For I am The Way."

It has always been easy for me to identify with the young father who brought his son to Jesus (*see* Mark 9:-17–27). It was obviously an impossible case. There was no hope—except Jesus. And Jesus said to the young father, "If thou canst believe, all things are possible to him that believeth." Even when the father had only one hope open to him, even when there was no alternative, he teetered on the brink of fearing to risk. He had to be honest:

> And straightway the father of the child cried out, and said with tears, Lord, I believe; help thou mine unbelief!
>
> Mark 9:24

Often the best we have to offer in our humanness is the "want to" of faith. But Jesus holds out His hands to us in love to take even our "want to's" when that's the best we can do. There are times when we may have to pray, *Lord, I don't feel like trusting; I don't feel like praying, but I* want *to want to.* Whatever we have, even if it's only our questions and doubts and uncertainties, if we will just abandon them to Him, He will take them. We don't have to have all the answers or solve all the problems or resolve all our doubts. But we do have to wrap them up and hand them over, choosing rather to know only The Way.

The young father gave it all to Jesus: his belief and his unbelief and his son. He let Jesus take all of them. "[And] Jesus took him [the boy] by the hand, and lifted him up; and he arose" (v. 27).

I suppose if Bill and I could have foreseen all it would involve when we committed our lives to the Lordship of Christ, we would not have been able to cope with it all—the joy and the pain, the excitement and the disappointment, but most of all the adventure. Often when we ask God to show us what lies in store, we are too dumb to realize we couldn't handle the glory of it without the endurance-building preparation of struggle. In our humanness it is so easy to gauge our spiritual progress by the way we feel. Those wonderful exhilarating moments, when we are permitted to view the valley from the mountaintop, can become habit-forming. The thin air can intoxicate our brains. If we're not careful, we will get fickle and flabby and self-indulgent, deciding that those extraordinary moments of inspiration should be par for the course.

In the light of the Word of God, I am a little afraid to demand miracles and the extraordinary, especially if, by "miracles," I mean temporal abundance and physical comfort. The words of Jesus demand a commitment that is not contingent on how we feel, what we have, or how sure we are of the final outcome. There is no place in the New Testament that suggests that after we have experimented with everything else, we should "try Jesus," implying that if that doesn't work to get us what we want, we could go on to something else. Quite the contrary, Christ's Way demands a total commitment of everything we have and are—sink or swim, live or die, rich or poor, sick or well. For example, physical healing is very much a part of our theology, but not everyone is healed. When Jesus brought physical healing, it was usually accompanied by a prayer which went something like this: "Father, that they may know that Thou has sent Me," or That Thy name may be glorified." The loaves and fishes, the wine at the wedding, and the miraculous healings were all ways of translating into a language we could understand that Christ's Kingdom was "not of this earth." If our commitment to follow Jesus is only based on the promise of "loaves and fishes," we're on dangerous ground. Redemption is reduced to a welfare program if we define Abundant Life in terms of fur coats and fine cars and lovely houses.

It's not that Christians should not have these things. It's just that whether or not we have them is beside the point. Our attitude toward what we have of material things is what matters. We must hold the things of earth with an open hand, letting them come and go without closing our fist.

When we come to Jesus we risk everything, commit it all for now and forever. We are no longer of this world. Things of this world become things we accept with gratitude or freely relinquish according to the ebb and flow of His perfect will.

Our life in Jesus Christ is a pilgrimage. Seasoned travelers travel light. They enjoy the trip but they make sure any treasures they accumulate on the journey can be shipped on ahead and will pass customs. They may camp out or stay in the finest hotels. They may run, walk, stumble, drive, or fly, but they never lose sight of the reason for the journey, and they never miss a chance to see a rainbow on the way.

> I believe, help Thou my unbelief.
> I take the finite risk of trusting as a child.
> I believe, help Thou my unbelief;
> I walk into the unknown, trusting all the while.

I long so much to feel the warmth
That others seem to know;
But should I never feel a thing,
I claim Him even so!

I believe, help Thou my unbelief.
I walk into the unknown,
Trusting all the while.
I walk into
   the
      unknown,
         trusting. . . .

Jesus Is Lord

We are discovering more and more each day the dimension in this New Life *beyond* forgiveness. By that I mean that beyond the relief in knowing that our sins are forgiven, beyond the initial "birth" into the Family of God, beyond the lifting of the burden of guilt there is *more,* so much more!

It distresses me to look back at my own life and see how long it took me to move into this new dimension, and I must admit that those days of struggle were some of the most miserable in my whole life. It is very painful to hang suspended between the discovery of a new and better way of life and the actual power to experience this New Life that one has discovered. I didn't want to go back— and I couldn't seem to go on. I loved the freedom of being forgiven and made new, and yet I was consumed with the constant struggle to be what this New Life demanded of me. But my "want to's" were always in conflict with the reality of what I actually was able to be in the mundaneness of my days.

I wanted more than anything to do always those things that are good and right in God's sight. But the list was so long and there were sublists to worry about—feeling proud that I was so truthful, analyzing my real motives for being so generous, or wondering whether it was goodness or cowardice that kept my virtue. There was no end to it.

I tried. Oh, how I tried! I was conscientious almost to a fault. I worried all the time about hurting someone's feelings, shading the truth, being loving and kind, giving of myself. I questioned myself at the end of every day. "Did I live like Jesus today?" And always, no matter how hard I tried, I always came up short. There was always that gray nebulous feeling that I had forgotten something here or not quite made it there. There was almost never that feeling of utter joy which I had so often heard people talk about.

But I didn't want to let go. I didn't want to go back to the days of guilt followed by periods of blanking it all out with the who-cares-anyway syndrome. I did care now. I had been freed from the past. I had been forgiven.

No wonder folks look at Christians and say, "If that's peace and joy and happiness, who needs it?" I was certainly not "bubbling all the time." I was nervous and uptight and afraid I would fail or fall short or be less than perfect—which, try as I might, I *was!*

When other Christians talked about sharing this wonderful New Life with others who were really hurting, I wanted to. But my "witness" was weak because there was always the nagging realization that I wasn't good enough myself that kept drawing my attention from the hurts of others to my own imperfections. When there was a chance for commitment in groups or at church, I always felt conviction myself, so I very seldom felt like praying or sharing with anyone else.

Most of the time there was nothing specific I could lay my finger on. There weren't any specific transgressions that I knew of, except things like words spoken too quickly or not quickly enough and attitudes or thoughts that came as a result of my own nervous reactions to others because of dissatisfaction with myself. Mainly, there was just that gray feeling that somewhere, somehow, I had missed the mark.

I don't even like to think about how long this went on. All during this time I heard people I admired speak of "letting go," "surrendering all," "total commitment," the "second blessing," the "infilling." I went through the motions of trying to get what they were talking about. There were many trips to the altar to find "sanctification" and all those other things. But when I returned to my world, the struggle went on.

Now, I'm sure that if I had been killed in an automobile crash during those days, I would have had "eternal life." But it wasn't the eternal life out there in eternity I was worried about. I needed desperately for *eternity* to invade my days right here. It was the quality of living in this world that was so poor. I know why some people who seem to have fairly decent circumstances spend so much time talking about "trials and tribulation in this vale of tears." But there are others who have lived through circumstances that seem to me to be hell on earth, yet they are often the ones who bubble and talk about the joy.

How I longed for whatever it was that *those* folks had that made them optimistic and joyful. I knew it was more than Pollyannaish, head-in-the-sand, pie-in-the-sky nonsense. Their circumstances did not allow them to indulge in the luxury of such an unrealistic philosophy. Whatever it was, I wanted it.

I asked for it. I prayed for it. I begged God for this power and this inner strength. I had heard preachers say that if we meet the conditions of God's promises, we have the right by faith to demand that God give us what He has promised. I demanded. The struggle went on.

Finally, weary and exhausted and sick of trying, I said something like, "I've had it!" I don't even know if it was a *bona fide* prayer or just a cry from the depths of my being. But the cry went something like this: "I'm sick of trying. I'm going to quit trying! I'm exhausted in my heart. I don't want to go back, but work as I may I can't get ahead. I'm giving it up. It's up to You. If You can't keep me, I'm finished with the struggle!"

There wasn't a flash of lightning or a voice from heaven. I didn't begin to speak in another language. There was only a quiet—somewhere in the very depths of my being. I remember once when I was fourteen we had a tornado in our little town. It was awful. But afterwards—after the wind and the roar that sounded like ten jet engines, after the churning of the debris, after the shouts of people running for safety, after it all—I went out on the sidewalk in front of our house. I'll never forget the silence! Louder than any sound. It was deafening. No one could fail to hear the quiet of that moment.

And I could not mistake the calm that I felt in my soul that day that followed the turmoil of my struggle to *be*. I had fought so hard and so long to hold on to the Abundant Life that had begun in me, terrified always that if I didn't hold on, it would somehow slip away through my fingers and be gone. But the peace I felt and the gentle, inner sigh of relief told me that the New Life I was trying so hard to protect was not as fragile as I had feared. It was tough and powerful enough so that when I quit my struggling, it could come to totally possess me. It wasn't something that I had to hold in a viselike grip like some prisoner I had by the throat. It was more like an energy that was infused into my very being, giving me the endurance and vitality to become what my highest aspirations and best efforts could never produce.

Yet I had stumbled over the simplicity of letting go. Perhaps it was necessary for me to come to the end of what I could do on my own. Maybe I'm a hardhead, or just plain slow to catch on. But whatever it was, Christ's power did not come into my life in its fullness until I gave up. I guess that is what God had been wanting for me to do all along.

Why is quitting the struggle so hard to do?

The other day I walked by the stairway where Benjy was standing about five steps up. "Hey, Mom!" he yelled. I turned just in time to see him flying through the air like some kind of missile hurled into space, coming right at me, perfectly convinced that I would throw out my arms and catch him. He was right! I did.

When Amy has a fever from strep throat or the flu, she opens her mouth wide to swallow any medicine I tell her will make her feel better. She trusts me. And I give her only those things that will make her well and strong.

Children trust. Children know how to abandon themselves to the strength and power of someone else who loves them. Why does it take us so long to catch on to that secret when we are children in God's Family?

Last summer on vacation Bill rented a large pontoon boat, and we all spent the afternoon cruising beautiful Lake Barkley in Kentucky. The rays of sunshine danced like mountain nymphs on the ripples in the water. From the pine and hardwood forests that mostly cover the Land-Between-the-Lakes, the calls of the birds—quail, mockingbirds, crows, and cardinals—echoed across the water, lulling the children to sleep on the blanket we had spread over the bow of the boat. I watched them, lying back in the security that the boat would get them across the lake and back to camp. They weren't Olympic swimmers, but that didn't keep them awake. They just trusted the boat.

If only we could be more like children in our faith. If only we could simply "trust the boat." *That's what faith is,* I thought—knowing we can't make it to shore but the boat *can.* It's learning to lie back in what God is, confident in the worthiness, not of our own frail hull, but of Him. It is not what we could ever do that counts; it is what He has already done. The thing that plugs us in to all that He is, is the daring to let go and lie back in His love.

I guess what had been happening in my life during these miserable years was really a struggle over the Lordship of my life. I have learned that it is one thing to accept Jesus as Savior and Redeemer and have our sins forgiven, and it is quite another thing to let Jesus come into our lives as Lord. And after that initial commitment to making Jesus our Lord, learning to practice the Lordship of Christ in our lives has been for Bill and me a continuing process. As we grow and mature in the things of the Spirit, there are always new areas of our lives about which we become aware that we have yet to commit fully to His Lordship. But, with each new experience of relinquishing our own control and letting the Holy Spirit move in, we gain courage and reinforcement for daring to do it again and again.

Sometimes I think it is easier for Bill to practice the Lordship of Christ than it is for me. He doesn't seem to have to take every single thing in his life one by one and go over the whole process of letting go. It seems that he just operates confidently, knowing that God is at work in his life and his judgment and his decisions. For him there is seldom a division between "secular" and "sacred." He has learned that all his decisions are, at the very core of the matter, spiritual decisions. In business relationships, in personal relationships, in church relationships, decisions and choices are molded by the discipline of the Lordship of Christ in his life.

For me it has been a case of an initial crisis experience in surrender, followed by numerous "refresher courses" in which I have had to reaffirm and apply my initial lesson to the new circumstances. As God shows me new areas of my life, I seem to have to say again and again, "Yes, Lord. That, too." The original general commitment to let go was honest and sincere. I meant to give Him full control, but the process of applying that to the specifics in my life goes on. But I'm learning.

This process of learning to let go and lie back in God's love has been for me a little like learning to swim. First of all, it's scary. You really can't even learn until you jump into water that is over your head. Someone else can show you all the strokes, and you can watch the form and ease of the best swimmers in the water. You can practice kicking your legs at the side of the pool, and you can wave your arms in the air, trying to imitate the strokes. You can even jump into the water and kick and flail around with all your might. You might even fight your way to the surface for air often enough to stay alive, but until you learn to relax and trust the water, you will only be a poor imitation of a swimmer—and a very exhausted one, at that! People are not born swimmers. They are limited because they are not sea creatures. But when a person stops fighting the water and learns to trust it, he finds that all those facts he has learned about water displacement and the laws of buoyancy are really true! Once he learns the reality of the facts for himself he can begin to relax. He begins to breathe and move to the rhythm of the waves, the ebb and flow of the tide. The more practice he has at this, the more natural it becomes. The breathing and movements of swimming become second nature, almost an instant reflex.

In much the same way, as we learn to lie back in the love of Jesus and submit to the rhythm of His very life in us, we become more and more secure in the knowledge that His laws of love are at work in our lives. We may have to adapt what we have learned to new situations. Swimming in a heated indoor swimming pool is not quite the same as swimming in the surf of the Atlantic Ocean. The endurance and skill and knowledge demanded may increase. But with each new experience, strength and confidence is built.

That first experience with letting go came for me when I was young and single. The things that worried me then were things like my relationship with my parents and my school friends, my choice of an educational direction, my associations at church, my dating relationships, the choice of a future mate, responsibilities at my high school, jobs, and things like that. Although my *commitment* at that time was total, I was not aware of what that commitment would demand of me later on, as I am now not aware of the specifics that yet lie ahead for me to place under the Lordship of Christ in the future.

It was the week of Amy's birthday in June, and she wanted to have a cookout down at the creek. She wanted to have hot dogs and hamburgers, corn on the cob, green beans, watermelon, and raspberry cake. The afternoon of the big affair, Grandma and Grandpa were the first to arrive. Benjy had a brand-new ball and bat and wanted Grandma to play ball with him. So while Amy waited for the cousins and the rest of us loaded the wagon, Benjy and Grandma went on down to play ball. As I came down the hillside with a pot of hot coffee, I could see them under the willow tree, Grandma pitching and Benjy up at bat. It was a lovely, heartwarming scene, and I was thinking how contented they both looked, when I saw Benjy throw his bat on the ground, stomp his angry little feet, and yell at the top of his lungs, "Grandma! You missed again! *You missed my bat again!*"

It turned out to be that kind of day for little Benjy. Nothing went the way *he* wanted it. He wanted it to be *his* birthday, but it was Amy's. He wanted to eat watermelon when we were roasting hot dogs. He wanted to go for a paddle-boat ride, but everyone else was running races. By the end of the day, with all the playing, running, fighting, and crying, Benjy was exhausted. He held his arms up at me and said, "Carry me, Mommy," so I carried him up the hillside to the house. He was all hot and dirty, and he went to sleep on my shoulder before I got him to the top. I took him to his room and laid him on his green bedspread. How dear he looked—his blond hair all plastered to his forehead, catsup on his nose, a grubby little baseball clutched tightly in one hand! How I loved him! I took the baseball from his little fingers and smiled to myself as I remembered what he had said earlier about missing his bat. Somehow, as I stood there beside that exhausted little boy, now holding his toy in my hand, I became aware of some struggles of my own, some areas in my life that I needed to relinquish—once more. There had been times when I had acted like a spiritual two-year-old. Times when I had stood with my own neat little set of needs and longings and desires in my hand, and in my own more subtle and sophisticated way "screamed" at my children and my husband and the church and others around me, "You missed my bat! Here I am, with my needs all ready to be met, *and you missed my bat.*" I recognized the weariness I was beginning to feel in my soul. I'd been there before. A weariness that comes from struggle over Lordship in an area of my life. Perhaps I had let it go on so long this time because it involved my children and Bill. I knew well that "he that would save his life would lose it." But it was not so easy to apply that principle to those dearest to me in all the world. Houses and lands and cars and plans—yes! My family? Not so easy. In my head I knew that, in holding them tightly, I might lose them forever. But in practice, I held them in little ways: making them need me, overburdening them with the awareness that I needed them—subtle little ways of keeping them for myself and my needs and my fulfillment.

So that day beside a sleeping little boy, I knelt and gave

it all up to Jesus: my precious children, my special husband, my hopes and plans and dreams and schemes, my fears and failures, all of it. Once more the peace and contentment came as the struggles ceased.

Since that day, the relationship of our household has grown more beautiful than ever, and running in and around and through it all is God's freedom to *be.* I should have known. When Jesus wins, everybody wins!

There will, no doubt, be other times, new things to place in His care, new lessons in openhanded living. As long as we live and grow there will be times to make specific the integrity of our commitment to the total Lordship of Christ in our lives. Bill and I have celebrated that Lordship in many songs. Perhaps this is the one that says it best:

> All my tomorrows, all my past—
> Jesus is Lord of all.
> I've quit my struggles, contentment at last!
> Jesus is Lord of all.
>
> King of kings!
> Lord of lords!
> Jesus is Lord of all.
> All my possessions, and all my life,
> Jesus is Lord of all.
>
> All of my longings, all my dreams—
> Jesus is Lord of all.
> All my failures His power redeems!
> Jesus is Lord of all.
>
> All of my conflicts, all my thoughts—
> Jesus is Lord of all.
> His Love wins the battles I could not have fought!
> Jesus is Lord of all.
>
> JESUS IS LORD OF ALL!

Yet I Will Praise Him

It was learning to let go and lie back in the love of Jesus that taught us the meaning of "praise." We had often heard Christians talk about praise and adoration. We had sung about it at worship in lofty songs and anthems. We had often heard it said that the reason God created man in the first place was so that man could praise Him and glorify His name.

But to tell you the truth, we didn't get it. Deep in our inner hearts we would reason that if God was God, the Creator of the universe, omnipotent, omnipresent, omniscient, and owner of the "cattle on a thousand hills," He certainly would not need to have us mere human creatures spend the span of life He Himself had allotted us just telling Him how great He is. We never breathed a word of our feelings in proper religious circles or hardly even to ourselves aloud, but it really sounded to us as if what we heard people describe as the "sole purpose of man" was egoism on the part of the Creator.

We were totally unable to fit this in with the things that Jesus—God's revelation of Himself to man—said and did. Jesus was a servant. He refused crowns and disappeared from throngs who wanted to enthrone Him. He washed people's feet and said that he that would be master must be servant of all. He scorned self-centeredness and condemned the Pharisees for seeking the praise of men. We could not understand why a trait that Jesus clearly taught was evil in our lives could be a virtue in God. Often we thought of the lines from "The Eternal Goodness" by John Greenleaf Whittier:

> Not mine to look where cherubim
> And seraphs may not see,
> But nothing can be good in Him
> Which evil is in me.

It wasn't a case of rebellion against God or being unaware of His power and might. We knew that God *was* God and worshiped freely the glory of His power to change our lives. It was the *praise* concept we could not understand, not that we didn't want to give praise, but that God would demand it and, in fact, create us just so that He could hear it. The way we heard it explained left God sounding like an insecure child who had to be constantly reassured of His worth and goodness or He would get angry and vent His wrath on all mankind in some horrible way for our ingratitude in having been created —albeit just to praise Him.

There's a bit of advice that my mother gave me while I was growing up which served us well during this time and helped to keep us from getting things out of focus until the Lord could teach us what He wanted us to know. She often said to me, "Gloria, don't throw out anything until you have something better to take its place." Many times that counsel has kept me from making too-quick judgments and "throwing the baby out with the bathwater." We realized that this praise business was a piece of the puzzle that didn't fit, so instead of throwing out the puzzle, we just waited until the growth in our lives could bring us to the place where we could clearly see how and where the piece belonged.

That time came soon after our discovery of the freedom in making Jesus "Lord of all." It began, as growth usually does, with new insight into the Word. It was a verse in Psalms: "But thou art holy, *O thou that inhabitest the praises of Israel.* Our fathers trusted in thee: they trusted, and thou didst deliver them" (22:3, 4).

I had taken enough biology in school to know about natural habitats. This verse was saying that God's habitat, God's place to dwell and live and function normally, was in "the praises of Israel." God lived in the praises of His people. Then that must mean that if we wanted God to have a place to live in and around our lives on a daily basis, we would have to create in this world (which is no "friend to grace") a place for Him to dwell. And He dwells in the praise of His people. It was praise that made a hollowed-out place, a hallowed place, in the midst of this evil world for God to live. If we wanted God to be a constant and permanent resident in our lives and in our days, we would have to maintain for Him a habitat.

That next part gave us a clue to how that was to be done. *Trust* was the word. "Our fathers *trusted* in thee: they *trusted,* and thou didst deliver them." Trust was just what we had been learning. Letting go. Lying back. Risking. Giving up what little we had in strength and power so that we could confidently relax in His power and strength. We were learning to trust.

Perhaps it was the risk of opening ourselves fully to the Lordship of Christ—the total childlike trust in Jesus—that was praise. Perhaps it was "openhanded" living that created a place for God to be. Perhaps *praise* was not so much a noise we made as a way we were to live.

A verse in Hebrews confirmed what the Holy Spirit was beginning to teach us:

> ... Jesus suffered and died outside the city, where his blood washed our sins away.
>
> So let us go out to him beyond the city walls [that is, outside the interests of this world, being willing to be

despised] to suffer with him there, bearing his shame. For this world is not our home; we are looking forward to our everlasting home in heaven.

With Jesus' help we will continually offer *our sacrifice of praise* to God by telling others of the glory of his name. Don't forget to do good and to share what you have with those in need, for such sacrifices are very pleasing to him [italics added].

Hebrews 13:12–16 LB

Just as God has no permanent dwelling place here, we, too—who have become His children through Jesus Christ —would find that this world is not our permanent home. This was a good thing, since this world is on a collision course and will one day burn itself out. But while we stayed here, though only temporarily, we could keep God with us by making a place for His Holy Spirit to dwell in our lives. And this place was to be made by the sacrifice of our praise which we give by living our gratitude, by sharing what we have found of eternal value in Jesus, and by touching lives as Jesus did with His goodness, love, and resources.

For the first time we began to understand why people often lift their hands with open palms when singing or praying words of praise to the Lord. It is a symbol of an openhanded way of living. It is a way of saying, "I love You, Lord. My hands and my life are open to You. Take whatever You need from me. Give me whatever You want me to have. I have learned that You are utterly trustworthy. So my lifetime—abilities, possessions, questions, future, past, children, husband, parents, relationships—everything is open and available to the ebb and flow of Your will."

So that was it! Praise was a place for God to be. A home place. A workshop for His Holy Spirit in the midst of our

lives. It was an atmosphere of total openness where He
could be free to do good things in and through our days.
It was a home office in a foreign country, a sanctuary, safe
place, and refuge for the rescue operations of the world.
God's habitat in us was to be our praise, our openhanded
commitment to His total Lordship.

Now new content was coming to us for the misunder-
stood statements about "praising God" as our reason for
being here. If the Holy Spirit was going to be at work in
this world, He would need a place to be and move and
work. Only those who had made Him Lord in their lives
could create for Him such a place. That place was made
by the praise, the sacrifice of our availability, our trust, our
gratitude, our love, our willingness to serve, our openness
to His New Life in us.

Praising God was not to be a set of empty words to feed
and appease a giant celestial ego. It was not just an empty
liturgy, mumbled mechanically during some isolated sixty-
minute span during a week. It was a total commitment
that engulfed every moment and demanded the vital in-
volvement of every nook and cranny of our being.

It was more than a way to use God to get what we
wanted. It was not a spiritual con game in which we
thanked God ahead of time for things we requested, so
that He would then be obligated to come through with
the blessings. It was not a way to get healthy, wealthy, or
wise in this world's eyes by thanking and praising God, a
case of I-tell-Him-He's-great and He-gives-me-what-I-
want. Indeed, the riches in Christ Jesus might not show up
in tangible blessings that the world could even see. But
the world would sense the unexplainable joy and optimism. It could notice the healthy attitudes and open spirit
and happy outlook.

We have begun to call this way of openhanded life-style
the "pilgrimage of praise," and what an adventure it is!
Here are some places it is leading us.

This life of praise is teaching us to hold our *time* with an open hand. As Jesus becomes Lord of our time, two things seem to be happening. First, we have had to become more disciplined, for time is not our own. We are beginning to learn that we are eternally responsible to God for the use of it, and the limited allotment we have here must be used wisely. Each new morning is an opportunity to realign our priorities for that day and to choose the things in which we will invest the resource of time. But God is teaching us something else about His Lordship of our time. We must hold even our best intentions, well-planned schemes, and disciplined schedules with an open hand. In the final analysis we must be ready to give priority to those things that have eternity in them.

When plans and schedules keep us from wasting time, they are our friends. But when they keep us from hearing the cry of a child or touching the pain in the heart of a neighbor or sharing the joy of a companion, they become our enemies, tyrants. We have had to let Jesus help us master the use of time and make us sensitive to voices that call for the priceless gift of our moments. Yes, even time must be held with an open hand.

We are learning to hold *possessions* with an open hand. Things that we have must be held so loosely that they are completely at His disposal. A house is not important except inasmuch as it is a place of warmth and shelter for those who need a place to nestle in. A cupboard stacked with food is important only in its ability to say, "You're welcome here. There is nourishment for your body and your soul available in this place." A yard is a good place to make people (including little people) feel loved and cared for. If there is a pool or a badminton set or a picnic table, the Lordship of Christ can turn them into a wonderful way to share and reach and love. An automobile can be a marvelous tool of service. It can take children to music lessons that will begin a song in their hearts. It can start a backyard Bible school or bring people together to study God's Word. It can take old people to doctors' appointments or the grocery store.

I have a friend whose special calling it is to serve God with her house. She doesn't sing or write or sew. But she listens better than anyone I know and can whip up a plate of peanut-butter-and-jelly sandwiches to feed little hungry mouths quicker than a flash. Because she's so easy to talk to, people go to her house to unload their burdens, to ask questions, to be loved back to wholeness, and to learn about her Lord. Jesus is in that house, and Deanie's house is her tool of ministry. I remember one time her little boy was working on some project in Bible School that required his telling how many were in his family. "Well, there's six of us," he said. "There's my dad, Johnny Carroll, and my mom, Deanie Carroll, and there's Marty Carroll and Penny Carroll and Eddie Carroll—that's me— and Jesus Carroll. Six!" Jesus lived at his house. He knew it, and all of us who retreat there on occasion know it, too.

Since Bill and I have found our contribution to the Kingdom to be mainly in the area of writing and communication, we have learned that Jesus must be Lord of our *ideas and thoughts.* These, too, must be held with an open hand. It is not always easy to bare one's soul on paper, in a song, or before a group of people. Sometimes the concepts that seem the most profound to us have had to be learned with great difficulty and have really cost us in terms of commitment and struggle. These lessons become very special and dear, and sometimes we want to hold them close and savor them for ourselves. Sometimes it is fear that makes us hesitant to share an idea. Some of the things the Holy Spirit has taught us we know will not be popular, because they demand so much or because they expose shoddiness in the lives of those who carefully maintain a façade of religiosity. In our humanness it is easy to shrink from including those concepts in a song or book for fear someone will be displeased or critical. For example, one of our driving passions is to help people see the beauty "in their own backyard," to notice the miracles of everyday life, to see the specialness of their own children and to value the treasure of a good marriage. When critics scoff at this and call us "sentimental" and "saccharine" and "old-fashioned," it is easy to smart from the criticism and become gun-shy about including such experiences when we share the story of what Christ can do. There is nothing that makes one quite so vulnerable as *creating.* The artist or writer must put all there is of himself into his work. (And just as sure as I confess to that, there will be someone sure to say, "You call yourself a *writer?*" and I will shake inside and swear off ink pens for a month.) But often those who have never dared to take such a risk are usually the severest critics. They are often the ones to analyze and dissect every flaw and pick apart and "read into" a writer's intentions. But the Lordship of Christ demands that we praise God by daring to hold our ideas and thoughts with an open hand, realizing that we are all still "kids under construction," and "the Lord might not be finished yet." One day He will no doubt lead us yet beyond the lessons we are now learning, but in the meantime we must be willing to share the struggle and victories of our pilgrimage along the way, reaching always toward the ways that are higher than our ways—and "His thoughts that are above our thoughts."

A life of praise calls us to hold an open hand on our *plans and dreams.* I have already told something about Bill's experience with letting God choose the direction his love for music would take him. Let me here share with you the rest of the story. After he returned home from singing with that quartet, he enrolled in college. Since it seemed that God was closing the door on the singing career he had dreamed of, Bill chose to major in English and only minor in music. This forced him to read and

study writers and poets and playwrights. It required him
to do some creative writing and verbalizing of his own.
This was not "fun and games" for him at the time, but it
was an alternative to the music he had "given up." To
satisfy his love for music, he sang with his little sister and
brother in churches on the weekends. The warm services
brought spiritual nourishment to his soul, as the discipline
of study began to sharpen the tools of communication.
Before long there were things Bill wanted to share on the
weekends, but there didn't seem to be songs available to
express those things he was growing to feel deeply in his
heart. He began to write—timidly, at first—about the joy
in serving the Lord and his own personal trip to Calvary.
The people responded to the things this young man was
sharing through his songs.

When Bill finished college, he began to teach English in
junior high school. If this was what God wanted him to do,
he would do it with gusto. His quick humor and his sensitivity to the chemistry of the classroom made him an
outstanding teacher and an easy favorite with the young
people who affectionately called him Mr. G. He loved
those kids, and they knew it!

After teaching junior high school for several years
and finishing at the same time a master's degree in
counseling, he wanted to try teaching in senior high
school and transferred to a position that had just
opened in his own hometown. He was still writing a
few songs, but his sister was now grown and starting a
family of her own, and his brother had moved away,
putting an end to the trio's singing. Instead, Bill began
to direct a church choir and organize other musical talent in the church.

It was at this point that I first met Bill. But let me begin
my story at the beginning, for I, too, had a set of dreams
and hopes that I was learning to hold with an open hand.
I wanted very much to discover God's will for my life. I

sort of had the idea that God's will was like a great big box with a red ribbon on it that I would one day stumble on if I walked the right path. Right away I would recognize it! GOD'S WILL FOR MY LIFE would be written all over it, and the box would include my husband (if I were to marry), a career and place of service, and all the answers to the questions of direction for my life. But in the meantime, I knew I must prepare as best I could for the day of this great discovery.

I shall be eternally grateful for wise parents. How often they reminded me that God's will was always my doing those things that I knew to be right for each day, and doing them the best I possibly could. So I tried to prepare. In those days there weren't many "Christian careers" open to a girl. She could either hope to marry a minister and be a preacher's wife or she could go to a foreign-mission field. If neither of those worked out, she could always teach. It was the foreign-mission work that seemed the most attractive to me, although I loved children and wanted to be open and ready for any possibilities. I knew it was God's will for me to be a good student and a good steward of my mind. That wasn't so glamourous, but it was something I *knew* to do. I knew it was important to keep my relationships honest and pure. That wasn't very glamourous sometimes, but it was something I *knew* to do. I really loved to write. I loved ideas and thoughts and concepts, and I found my greatest fulfillment in those classes that required writing and verbalizing abstract thoughts. English and literature and speech and philosophy were the areas on which I concentrated, in case teaching might be my place. But in trying to be obedient to the possibilities, I also took three years in high school and a major in college of a foreign language—French.

So the days passed. All the while I was watching for the big box with the red ribbon, not realizing that "God's Will

for My Life" was not a "thing" to be discovered on my
path, but the *path* itself, a pilgrimage in trust and obedience in which each new day was to be the fulfillment of
all previous preparation—and at the same time the preparation for all things yet to come.

It was my junior year of college. I was just going along,
doing with all my energy what I *knew* to do for each day.
I had an unusually heavy load that semester, eighteen
hours of classes and two part-time jobs; but one day after
French class my professor called me in and asked me if I
could go over to Alexandria and teach some classes. It
seems that the French teacher there was to have a serious
operation that would keep her out of classes for about
seven weeks. No qualified language teacher could be
found, so the high school had called the college to see
whether some advanced students could fill in. Another
girl and I could split the classes and fit them into our
schedules. Partly because of the challenge and partly because I needed the money for tuition, I consented to go.
I was to begin the first day of the second semester—the
same day Bill transferred to the new challenge of high
school.

It was in the high-school office that we met, and soon
we began to see each other at noon or after school to
share ideas and philosophy and values. It was a long
time before he mentioned music, and longer still before he hinted that he was writing some. By then we
were dating seriously and had discovered more than
enough about each other to make us both convinced
we wanted to spend our lives together. It was the summer before we were married, and I was working at
home (in Battle Creek, Michigan, sorting cornflakes)
that he found out about my writing. It was a summer
of letters and notes and poems, and it was a very special experience for us both to have to verbalize our
growing love in black and white—on paper—in concrete terms. (Every couple should be lucky enough to

have to spend some time apart writing letters.)

Needless to say, neither of us could have foreseen what has happened since in this marvelous adventure of serving Jesus together. Bill's music and my writing have found their way to the surface of our lives in ways more beautiful and exciting than we could ever have dreamed.

And I am convinced that our blind efforts at obedience were the very things that God honored and used to bring us together in a very special ministry we could never have planned. The discipline of Bill's choice to study literature and poetic devices and writing styles gave him the tools he would one day use to share his love of music. And my years of studying foreign language in the most disciplined way I knew, brought me to Bill—and if I never use French again, God has let me know that He will use whatever we commit to Him to bring good into our lives.

Perhaps I should add a postscript to all of this. God has allowed Bill a growing ministry not only in writing, but in singing from coast to coast, and God has used our songs to the point that they are now being translated into many languages and recorded and sung around the world. That French is coming in handy, after all!

And if you should ever ask Bill Gaither to sign his name for you on a record or sheet of music, he will probably write, beneath his name "Romans 8:28," the motto of openhanded praise-living:

> And we know that all things work together for good
> to them that love God, to them who are the called
> according to *his* purpose.

Bill and I received a letter not long ago that said, "I don't understand your song 'Let's Just Praise the Lord.' Why do you say *'just'?* That doesn't make any sense to me—*just* praise the Lord." That same week there was a letter from a young mother who had buried their

nine-year-old daughter a few days before. She said,
"Our daughter was with us at your concert a year ago,
and we sang together as a family with you, 'Let's Just
Praise the Lord.' I didn't fully realize then why you
say, 'Let's *Just* Praise the Lord,' but I do now. Sometimes we *just* go on praising the Lord, when there's
nothing else to do."

Our lives, our possessions, our plans, our dreams, our
families, our children, our houses and lands, our time, our
talents—we hold in our open hands. We raise those hands
in praise to Jesus who "freely giveth all things," realizing
that His ways *are* higher than our ways, and His thoughts
higher than our thoughts. Drawn by the sweet aroma of
the sacrifice of our praise, He will come to dwell and make
His home in the open air of the tabernacle of our days.
We'll know no fear, for we can trust Him—who doeth all
things well.

When He's been at home in us, we're sure to feel at
home with Him.

There may be times when I have all life has to offer,
And there may be times when I have nothing to claim.
Though I may taste of poverty and taste of riches,
Yet through it all, I'll praise His name.

Though all my plans and hopes may seem reduced to ashes,
Though ev'ry dream I've dreamed may flicker and die,
The spirit's breath will flow across the smold'ring embers—
Rekindle again, consuming fire!

When the Parade of Saints shall reach its destination
Shall stand in white at last before the throne,
I'll be no stranger standing in His loving presence:
For I've been His child, and I'll feel right at home.

Yet I will praise Him!
The sweet Rose of Sharon,
The Lion of Judah,
The Desert's cool Spring,
Foundation of Zion,
The Star of the morning
The Hope of the ages—My God! and my King!

IV

Because He Lives . . .

His body is a living, breathing organism, commissioned to carry healing to a sick world.

Getting Used to the Family

I've had a little trouble arranging the order of the chapters in this book, and, you know, the more I think about it, the more I think there's good reason for that. The reason, I think, is this: No two people come to Jesus by the same process, and no two lives in the Spirit grow alike. We in the church like to think that there's a nice, neat growth pattern and everyone had better fit into it. Sometimes we are very hard on the newborn who doesn't seem to be passing through the stages in the chronological order we have ingrained in our spiritual brains. But when Paul said, "Work out your salvation with fear and trembling" (*see* Philippians 2:12), I think he meant just that. And it seems to me that this statement puts a lot of the responsibility for the process of growing on the *grower,* not on the rest of the trees in the orchard. The other trees have all they can do to keep the sap flowing to their own branches, because if they don't, the gardener will lop off those branches that don't produce.

I think that sometimes new Christians get so bogged down trying to fit into all the patterns in all the minds of all the saints, that they can't keep the lines clear for the Holy Spirit to work on their *very* individual points of need. Like human children, the young "child of God" is tender and sensitive and easily convicted. He is also easily bruised and beaten down and discouraged. Just because we older Christians can make him feel guilty by bringing up areas of needed growth, it doesn't necessarily mean that the Holy Spirit has brought the young Christian to the place in his personal process of maturing where he is ready to deal with that aspect of his life. On the other hand, he may be growing by leaps and bounds at some point of inferior maturity in *our own lives.*

Mark Twain once said that it wasn't the things he didn't understand about the Bible that bothered him; it was the things he *did* understand. The point is that there's enough stuff there to keep us all busy for a millennium, if we had that much time, so our energies need to be focused on encouraging each other and helping to create an environment in which we can all do as much growing as possible, by whatever process the Holy Spirit sees fit to tailor-make for our best good.

Bill often says that, while he was growing up in the church, he used to hear people talk and testify and preach —longingly—about going to heaven, a place where we're going to live forever and forever—with a whole bunch of people that we can't get along with down here. We may smile at that, but as my dad always used to say, "It's more truth than poetry!" All too often we spend more time griping than grappling and growing.

I think part of the reason for this is that somewhere between the New Testament and the twentieth century there has been a shift in our subconscious definition of what we now call "the organized church." The church of the New Testament was the fellowship of believers in which people who had chosen to risk their lives on the belief in Jesus Christ as Master and Lord (*the* Church) came together to share their needs and weaknesses and heartaches. It was here they gained strength to go out to be sharers of the Good News.

But gradually, the church has become the place we hold lectures about God and Christ and religion, and if anyone out there in the world wants help, he is to come to our building, listen to our sermons, walk the aisles to our altars, and accept our Lord. We don't go to him any-more; he has to come to us. And the church has become the place of evangelism. There's nothing so terribly wrong with that, except too often it forces the church folk to "look good" for the "lost" who come to our services.

I believe that there were some definite advantages to the New Testament way. The Christian has problems and needs and faults and failures, like anyone else. No use pretending he doesn't. But with Jesus as Lord of our lives, we have also a solution, a cure, and a pardon. So the church should be the loving fellowship where we can come with our frayed edges, our bruised elbows, our fail-ures and needs—and be knitted back together, bandaged up, prayed for, and loved back to wholeness. Then we could go out and show the world our lives, healed and whole and attractive. But instead we bring our nice faces and our phony façades to church, never giving a hint that we're falling apart on the inside, that we failed this week, that we're less than conquerors, because we don't want the "unsaved" to see our seamy side. But they *do* see it. Not in church, but on Monday morning when we go back to the pressures, discouraged, unraveled, and still carry-ing the load from the week before.

Now, I know each of us may come with boldness to the throne of grace at any time. But sometimes we just need the strength of some brother or sister, who really loves us and loves Jesus, to help pray us through a hard time.

And to tell you the truth, I don't think we fool anybody by our united front in the pew. We just set precedents for ourselves so that more and more we build ourselves pretty gilded cages we can't break out of. It gets harder and harder to tackle our inner problems, for they go un-confessed and not dealt with until the backlog looks like a mountain too big to climb. Of course, the outgrowth of all this is: "If we look so good in the pew, how come our lives show flaws?" Criticism begins. Accusations of "hypocrisy." Picking at young Christians. Having "fried preacher" for Sunday dinner. And the problem is not that there *are* flaws and faults and failures. (Let me whisper this so as not to shock anybody.) *We all have them.* It's denying that they exist when, during the week, folks can see that they *do* exist. And the flaws grow instead of disappear, because they are never dealt with within the loving fellowship of the Body of Christ.

If we were sure that we were loved—no matter what— in the Fellowship of Believers; if we could know that no matter what seamy side we had to unravel, the Family of God would love us anyway—if we really believed that our self-worth depends, not on what we've done, but on what He's done—then we could dare to tear away the layers of self-protection and get down to the wounds that need to be healed.

It seems that the Family of God is not so different from any other family. As the old saying goes, "You can choose your friends, but you're stuck with your family." In a way, that is true of the Family of God. We may as well quit acting as if there were an option of choosing whom we want to like and help and fellowship with in the church. We may as well accept the fact that the *Father* chooses who will be in the Family and it's up to us to be a brother or a sister to *anyone* who is a son or daughter of the Father.

Bill and I have three children. They are, like most children, bundles of contradictions: laughter–tears, giggles–tantrums, good days–bad days, endearing thoughtfulness–gross rudeness, glowing achievements–miserable failures, extraordinary uniqueness–mundane conformity. They are, in short, normal children. In trying to rear them, Bill and I try to be guided by a very simple philosophy: Deal with the rough edges while the children are still in the loving atmosphere of the home, because if *we* don't, the world out there will *knock* those edges off. We, as parents, would like to help them face and solve their problems, correct their faults, and develop their abilities in a place where they don't have to earn the right to be loved. At home each child is loved whether he deserves it or not; he doesn't have to earn it. He is loved just because he *is*, because he belongs to the family. We love the line from "The Death of the Hired Man" by Robert Frost that says that home is "something you somehow haven't to deserve." This is the atmosphere in which a child can dare to risk learning the disciplines of life. This is the place where he can fail—and not be a failure.

The home is, then, a place where the child is lovingly disciplined in a way that does not threaten his value as a person. The discipline is concentrated on correcting the problem without undermining the personality, so that the child feels assurance that correction does not mean rejection. At our house quite often we find ourselves saying, "We care what you do because we love you. If we didn't care, it wouldn't matter what you do."

The alternative to this is painful, sometimes fatal. If a child is allowed to go from the home unchallenged, undisciplined, and undeveloped, he will enter—unprepared— a world that will *not* love him just because he *is*. A young person so unprepared is likely to be buffeted, destroyed, and devoured by the world.

I would not be much of a parent if I pretended to "love my children too much to discipline them." I would not be doing them any favor if I rationalized my failure to take my responsibility seriously by claiming that I wanted my child to develop freely with no demands or restrictions. Such a claim would be at best very naive and at worst very cruel, for it would leave our children unprepared to cope adequately with unknown situations. What begins as permissiveness and evasion may turn out to be infanticide.

In the same way, it is in the Fellowship of Believers that we dare to let our flaws show and find the courage to deal with them. It is here that we do not have to act or look certain ways to be loved and undergirded and accepted. *We are valued because of Jesus' work of redemption on the cross.* The continuing work in the lived-out life of the believer can go on in this very favorable environment of patient love and nurture. Our Lord God is the Father who, by the Holy Spirit, brings to our spiritual consciousness the areas of needed growth. The brothers and sisters give us encouragement and strength by sharing their victories and needs.

Perhaps one reason we don't all grow alike is so that we can help each other. Maybe an area of weakness for *you* is an area in which God has just helped *me* gain some strength. Maybe an area of weakness for *me* is a place of past growth for *you.* Surely, no one would be arrogant or condescending in his attitude toward another fellow struggler. It is, after all, the Holy Spirit who brings to our consciousness the things we need to work on, and He is also the One who gives us the power to conquer those problem places.

Can you imagine the strength of a Family like that? Can you imagine how attractive it would be to the waifs of the world? The orphans? The battered children? How wonderful to have a home where you could be loved and fed and cared for and defended! To have a place where you could dare to expose your faults and fears and failures, a place where discipline and disapproval would never threaten your feelings of personal worth and acceptance! The Family at its best!

I wish we could read together the whole twelfth chapter of Hebrews. But let me pull out some very special lines and then perhaps you could go on and read the rest. I just want you to know that this Family I have described isn't something I dreamed up. It is the way God intended it to be. It was to be the place where all true children of God could grow strong in order to share the cure they had found with a dying world.

. . . let us strip off anything that slows us down.
. . . Keep your eyes on Jesus, our leader and instructor.
. . . And have you quite forgotten the encouraging
words God spoke to you, his child? He said, "My son,
don't be angry when the Lord punishes you. Don't be
discouraged when he has to show you where you are
wrong. For when he punishes you, it proves that he
loves you. . . . [that] you are really his child."

Hebrews 12:1, 2, 5, 6 LB

Try to stay out of all quarrels. . . . Look after each
other so that not one of you will fail to find God's
best blessings. . . .

Hebrews 12:14, 15 LB

Since we have a kingdom nothing can destroy, let
us please God by serving him with thankful hearts,
and with holy fear and awe. . . . Continue to love
each other with true brotherly love.

Hebrews 12:28; 13:1 LB

And from Colossians:

Don't tell lies to each other. . . . In this new life [in
Christ] one's nationality or race or education or social
position is unimportant; such things mean nothing.
Whether a person has Christ is what matters, and he
is equally available to all. . . . Don't worry about making
a good impression. . . . Be gentle and ready to forgive;
never hold grudges. . . . Most of all, let love guide your
life, for then the whole church will stay together in
perfect harmony. . . . And always be thankful.

Colossians 3:9, 11–15 LB

Going together, enjoying the trip,
Getting used to the Family I'll spend eternity with;
Learning to love you, how easy it is—
Getting used to the Family of God.

Climbing the mountains, crossing the plains,
Fording the rivers, sharing the pains;
Sometimes the losses, sometimes the gains—
Getting used to the Family of God.

Now, those are two verses of the little song Bill and I wrote about all this. It's a sweet, gentle sort of song that's fun to sing. It has a kind of easy rhythm to it. It feels like the easy rhythm of regular, routine days in a happy home. But I stopped here to get your attention before you go lilting on through the next verse. I wanted to tell you that the reason that a regular, routine day in a happy home gently sings its way along through the hours is not as simple as it seems when you happen to walk in at 5:30 P.M. and sit down at the kitchen table for supper. The "model child" you see got to be a "model child" as the result of a lot of not-so-model moments. The kitchen sparkles because somebody scrubbed it, and the lovely lady serving supper, humming a tune as she dishes up the mashed potatoes, *didn't look like that* when she was on her hands and knees making the kitchen *look like that*.

What I'm saying is that the fine moments in the family or the Family are the result of a process that includes a lot of hard work, patience, and just plain old nitty-gritty.

Now let's focus on the child for a moment. His pious moment, with his hair combed and his teeth brushed and his napkin neatly in place *began* somewhere else.

Many a baby Christian never reaches the moments of shining achievement—because some older Christian in the Family isn't willing to invest himself in the process.

Bill and I get so many letters from people who wasted half of their lives in sin—because years ago as fledgling Christians they got pecked and picked at and criticized right out of the nest by some "old hen" before they could even fly.

There are some very strong words of Jesus that make me think we'd better take the nurturing process very seriously:

> But whoso shall offend one of these little ones which believe in me, it were better for him that a millstone were hanged about his neck, and that he were drowned in the depth of the sea.
>
> Matthew 18:6

Jesus was talking about how we are to be like children if we are ever to get into the Kingdom of Heaven. Sometimes we who have been "in The Way" a long time tend to forget the process of our own pilgrimage and become so callous and legalistic that our judgmental attitudes outweigh our rightness. The tenderness and childlike, wide-eyed wonder can slip away, and we can become armed estate keepers instead of loving members of the Family.

"Give a warm welcome to any brother who wants to join you, even though his faith is weak," writes Paul. "Don't criticize him . . ." (Romans 14:1 LB).

Well, with all that heavy stuff in mind, let's happily sing our way through another day in the life of the Family—

> Reaching our hands to a brother who's new,
> Learning to say that *I really love you;*
>   [That's not so hard to say, is it?]
> Learning to walk as the Father would do—
> Getting used to the Family of God.

May God who gives patience, steadiness, and encouragement help you to live in complete harmony with each other—each with the attitude of Christ toward the other.

Romans 15:5 LB

It's a simple little song we wrote, but please don't mistake its simplicity for lightness. We're very serious about the message. Jesus said, "Love one another." It was a commandment, not an option. He is our Oldest Brother, the Firstborn of the Father. He has shown us how to treat each other. When in doubt about how we should act toward another member of the Family, we'll just have to treat him or her as Jesus did. Jesus said, "I love you"—with a cross. If we're serious about cure-sharing, we are going to have to live with each other in the Family in love and harmony. If we don't, the world will die, for others will never trust us to take them to the Great Physician.

The Family of God

There is a lot of humor in the Bible, and I just can't help chuckling to myself when I read some of the illustrations which Jesus and the apostles used to make things clear to us. Sometimes the mental images they create are enough to entertain our imaginations for hours. One of my favorites is found in First Corinthians and has to do with the Fellowship of Believers. It compares us to a body—as Jesus also did—but this description is very explicit. It begins: "For the body is *not one member,* but many"

(1 Corinthians 12:14).

Now right away I know what Benjy, our little boy, would see. His version would go something like this: "Once upon a time there was a B–I–G Eyeball. And it came rolling down the street, *bumpity, bump, bump,* down the curbs, along the sidewalk, and up to the ice cream shop. There he met a Big Mouth. Mr. Mouth said to Mr. Eyeball, "Well, imagine meeting you here! What are you doing at the ice-cream shop? You can't eat ice cream!" As the story develops, so does Benjy's imagination—and before you knew it there would be a council meeting with all the people in town—Mr. Foot, Miss Ear, Ellen Elbow, Tommy Great Toe, Nellie Kneecap, to name a few—to decide by majority vote whether or not to close the ice-cream shop.

Now, Benjy's version may be a little far-out for you, especially if you haven't recently had close contact with the workings of the mind of a first-grader. But even if you're not up to accepting his embellishments, you'll have to admit that the picture the Apostle Paul paints is not so different. Let's read it:

> If the foot says, "I am not a part of the body because I am not a hand," that does not make it any less a part of the body. And what would you think if you heard an ear say, "I am not part of the body because I am only an ear, and not an eye"? Would that make it any less a part of the body? Suppose the whole body were an eye—then how would you hear? Or if your whole body were just one big ear, how could you smell anything?
>
> 1 Corinthians 12:15–17 LB

See? Benjy wasn't so far off, after all! Now, I just can't help making some hypothetical applications of this illustration to the ways we Christians—the Body of Christ—

sometimes operate our religious organizations. It seems to be human nature for us to get hung up on certain functions of that special Body, forgetting that *any* body must work in its entirety if it is to be healthy and whole.

Some of us, for instance, operate as if we thought the Body were just one big digestive system. Our total attention is focused on ingestion and digestion: get more ideas, more approaches, more methods; learn long lists of 'how-to's'; devise more theories; secure more materials and equipment; memorize Scripture and commandments and creeds and theologies. *Take in, take in, take in.*

Sometimes we operate as if we thought the Body were just one big kidney—*purify, purify, purify.* We talk holiness and perfection and self-denial and the second blessing and sanctification and being "a peculiar people." We look askance at those who have only "been saved"—and say they are shallow and carnal and living below their privilege.

Some of us function as if we thought the whole Body were one big brain. Everything in spiritual life must be rational and objective. We accept nothing that smacks of emotion or subjectivity. All that we accept as "faith" is simply an applied system of reason, and even "testing the spirits," as we are commanded to do, is interpreted to mean that we simply measure people and situations by our own criteria, and if they meet the qualifications, then we accept them.

Sometimes we behave as if we thought the Body were just one great big heart—*love, love, love.* Accept everything. No restrictions, no discipline, no guidelines. Everything is evaluated by how it feels. Never deal with problems. Never make difficult decisions. Never mind that the Word of God is "quick and sharper than any two-edged sword." Just love and feel and avoid at any cost difficult confrontations with what the Lordship of Christ demands of us in behavior, life-style, and value judgments.

There are times when we behave as if we thought the Body were just a reproductive system. Having babies is all that matters. Our whole existence is for the purpose of conceiving and giving birth to more "babes in Christ." Never mind what happens to them after they're born. Just win more souls. Report more births.

Some of our organizations function as if we thought the Body were all muscle. Activity, sports, and movement are the purposes of the Body—*do, do, do.* Plan more ball teams, more bowling leagues, more teen nights, more wiener roasts, more men's breakfasts, more ladies' circles, more children's programs, more activities for the golden-agers. Have the most active church in town. Flex those muscles, cover more territory—*move, move, move.* It's like a giant spiritual Olympia Health Spa and Figure Salon.

But the Scriptures suggest that we are not to be organizations—but that the Body of Christ is a total being made up of various functioning and totally interrelated organs. Together we are an organism—not an organization. Together we all perform our various functions that keep the whole Body healthy and growing. For example, the heart is a vital organ of the *physical* body. It pumps nourishment to every muscle and cell of the body. It sends life to every organ. But without the blood to pump, it would pump air or nothing at all. Without the lungs to bring essential oxygen to the blood and without the cleansing action of the kidneys, the heart would pump poison to the whole body. If the purifying process did not happen, it would be fatal to the whole body.

Eating nourishing food is important to a body. But it is the brain that tells us which things are nourishing and which are lethal. We can't eat just *anything.* The brain, then, is the part that chooses for us those things that are good and will satisfy. But it, too, is dependent on the digestive system to break down and assimilate the food, and on the heart and lungs and kidneys to keep it alive with the nutrients that give it in turn the ability to go on making wise nutritional decisions.

Reproduction is important to the survival of the species. But if we are to have healthy, intelligent babies, one's body must be mature—grown-up enough to have met its own nutritional needs and to have some surplus for the nurturing of an offspring. It must be mentally and emotionally able to make wise choices and to protect and nurture a newborn. Poor general health, malnourishment, kidney poisoning, heart failure, poor judgment, anemia, and inertia can produce a diseased or crippled fetus or, in some cases, a stillborn. So it is important for the body to be able and willing to care for and nurture a newborn to a maturity of its own.

So it is in the Body of Christ; we are all members together. None of us functions or stays alive separate from or independent of the rest of the Body. It is the LIFE of Jesus Himself that is in us. "In him we live, and move, and have our being . . ." (Acts 17:28). For we are "alive with his life" (*see* John 1:4 NEB). So, in a very real way, Jesus Christ is still here on this earth in a visible, tangible form: the Body of Christ—walking, moving, loving, lifting, breathing, giving, healing, helping—for those who have been born into Him *are* His Body. No wonder Jesus said, "Your strong love for each other will prove to the world that you are my disciples" (John 13:35 LB). It is the perfection of the way the Body works together, hangs together, and reaches out together that proves to the whole world that Jesus is alive—for His Body is alive with His LIFE.

There is another beautiful part of that chapter about the Body:

> . . . we cannot get along without the parts of the body that seem to be weaker, and those parts that we think aren't worth very much are the ones which we treat

with greater care; while the parts of the body which
don't look very nice receive special attention, which
the more beautiful parts of our body do not need. God
himself has put our bodies together in such a way as to
give greater honor to those parts that lack it. And so
there is no division in the body, but all its different
parts have the same concern for one another. *If one
part of the body suffers, all the other parts suffer with
it; if one part is praised, all the other parts share its
happiness* [italics added].

1 Corinthians 12:22–26 TEV

I love that! When one suffers, we all suffer. When one
is praised, we all share the joy! Bill likes to illustrate this
to our kids by showing them his kneecap. It is the ugliest,
boniest, knobbiest kneecap you have ever seen. But suppose something happened to that kneecap! Last winter
his Aunt Maimie fell on the ice and broke her kneecap
right in two. The tendons snapped, the bone caved in, the
arteries ruptured, and for the whole winter she has been
in casts and braces. Now she is beginning ever so slowly
to stretch and bend the knee again. Nobody has to tell her
that the kneecap is an important part of her body. For
many weeks that kneecap has had the undivided attention of her whole self, because when one member suffers,
the whole body suffers. I doubt if ever in her life she'd
even given that kneecap a thought—until now. Important
part of the body? You bet!

I went outside this morning. I couldn't help it! Spring
was scampering all around the yard, mischievously blow-
ing its breath in little puffs at every budding twig and
hesitant daffodil as it passed. The ripples on the pond
were playfully tickling the belly-feathers of the ducks, and
the birds were giggling and flirting with each other. Joy
was in the offing. If all I could have taken with me to the

yard had been my nose, it would have still been glorious!
Smells I had forgotten through the winter accosted me at
every turn: the scent of damp, freshly thawed soil, sprout-
ing grass, forsythia in bloom, the water tumbling over the
dam, fresh from its icy prison. I came inside—giving
thanks for my nose. It had brought joy to my whole body.
My mind was clearer, my lungs felt expanded, my legs felt
like running and skipping—all because my nose had told
the rest of me that spring was here at last.

In the Body of Christ we are essential to each other. We
function as a living, pulsating organism. We can't chop
each other off or shove each other out. We need each
other. We are a part of one another. We are Christ to the
world—His very Self, His Body. If one part is injured or
missing, it cripples us all.

> Don't want to spend my time
> Praying prayers bombarding heaven
> With requests to rain down fire on Saints who care.
> In our method we may differ,
> But if Christ the Lord we live for,
> May we not forget the enemy's—
> OUT THERE!
>
> I want to spend my life
> Just making my part of the body
> Of the Savior work with smooth efficiency.
> One may be knee and one the nose,
>   You're the fingers . . . I'm the toes,
>   But, listen, brother,
>   *We have need of thee!*

Our local church is kind of regular; probably a lot like
yours. We have all kinds of people: young people, children, singles, couples, the middle-aged, old folks. We have

altos and sopranos and tenors and basses and monotones. We have "big mouths" and "timid souls," leaders and followers. We have weak Christians and giants of faith. We have some with the gift of insight, some with the gift of helps. There are some who can verbalize great truths and others who can't express the deep things of the Spirit at all. There are some with pleasant, delightful personalities and some who are abrasive and difficult to understand. There are tall people, short people, fat and skinny people, beautiful people, plain people, smart people and simple people. But the one thing that brings us together and causes us to leave our homes and separate lives is the pull of our common commitment to Jesus Christ.

I would not try to tell you that there aren't disagreements and differences within the fellowship. Some of us get impatient with the growth and maturing of others. Sometimes it seems as though a few are doing more work than others, pulling more of the load, taking more responsibility. Sometimes there are little flare-ups of criticism and resentment. But most of all, in and around and through and under it all, is a quiet knowing that we are all growing in some area or another and that God will deal with us individually and on His own terms, and that maturity will come if we can just feed and support and protect and be patient with each other. We are coming to realize in our fellowship that others are having to be patient with each of us. I personally am becoming more and more aware that there are blind spots and areas of unconquered territory in my life and that if I want the members of the Body to help compensate for my weaknesses, I'd better help "take up the slack" for someone else. This give-and-take in the Fellowship of Believers goes beyond our local fellowship. It includes the whole of the Body. But I can see the way it works most clearly in the part of the fellowship that is closest to home. (Let's hope we never become afflicted with the serious disease of myopia—nearsightedness—so that we think the segment closest to our nose is the *only* part of the Body that exists.)

Could I share with you a story of the Body at work? There is a young couple in our fellowship named Ron and Darlene Garner. They have three little children, just as Bill and I do. They are sort of a regular family with joys and sorrows, victories and defeats—about like the rest of us. They help carry the load of the church in whatever ways their particular abilities allow.

It was the Saturday after Good Friday that Ron went in for work at the garage where he was serving as a mechanic. He was working alone that day because he was making up time that he had taken off the previous Thursday to take his little daughter for some tests prior to some anticipated heart surgery. With the operation coming up, he knew they would need the money for hospital and doctor bills. While Ron was working with combustible material, there was an explosion. He managed to crash his way through the large double doors before the building blew apart and went up in flames, but he was severely burned over most of his body.

The news from the emergency ward in Muncie was indeed pessimistic: Ron was alive but was not expected to make it through the night. It was only minutes before a chain of telephone calls alerted the Family of God, and the whole church began to pray for Ron. All day long they prayed. Little groups, bigger groups, in homes, at the church, over the phone—all over town prayed the people who were related to Ron and Darlene because of Jesus. By evening the word came that, although the doctors gave no hope, Ron was still alive. They couldn't understand how he was holding on, but they said that, now that he had lived eight hours, possibly, if he could make it until morning, there was a chance—just a chance.

The Family kept on praying. Old folks prayed alone in their rooms. Children prayed in simple faith. Women prayed as they went about the tasks of caring for their families. Men prayed together in basements and over store counters and in automobiles. The church building was kept open, and lights burned all through the night as a steady stream of folks who cared and loved came to talk to Jesus about this young father who was "bone of their bone and flesh of their flesh."

The sun streamed in the windows that Easter morning on a sanctuary filled with the most weary, bleary-eyed congregation you've ever seen. There were very few Easter bonnets or bright new outfits. We were just there, drawn together closer than we had ever been before by the reality we had been sharing—that when one part of the Body suffers, we all suffer with it.

Nobody felt much like celebrating. There was hurt and there was pain in the Body, and that pain had drawn the attention of every other member. About twenty minutes into the service, the pastor came in with a report from the hospital. Although he had gone without sleep to be with the Garner family through the long hours, there was sunshine in his eyes. "Ron has outlived the deadline. The doctors say he has a chance. They are going to begin treatment."

For the Body of Christ, that news was better than eight hours of sleep and a good breakfast. New life was infused into us all. Tears of praise and joy began to flow, and our hope and gratitude poured itself into the glorious songs of Easter. "Jesus lives, and because He lives, we too shall live!"

Those songs that day were for us songs of commitment, too. We knew that the long, hard days for Ron and Darlene and the children had only just begun. With the words of victory we pledged ourselves to the reality of what would lie ahead: help with the children, many long trips to the hospital, pints of blood for transfusions, money for the astronomic hospital bills, meals to be taken to the family who would be too tired to cook, long months of support while the slow skin grafting and healing process went on. We knew what it would mean, and in our celebration we pledged ourselves to whatever it would take to make that injured part of the Body whole and well again.

On our way home from church that morning we were so full of the beauty of it all that we could hardly speak. Finally, we said to each other what we had come to realize through all of this: "They'd do that for us, too!" It was almost too grand to realize, but it was true! We aren't very model church members. The function we fill in the Body of Christ takes us away from a lot of the activities of our congregation. We're never available on Fridays and Saturdays. We get in early on Sunday mornings in time to get our children ready and to their Sunday school and church, but we can't be counted on to teach a class with a schedule like that. We always miss the fish fries, and I'm never there to make cakes and pies for the bake sales. But they'd do the same thing for us if *we* were the part of the Body that was suffering! Not because we were worthy or had earned special treatment or were indispensable—but just because we were a part of the Family of God!

As I started dinner, Bill sat down at the piano. Suzanne was skipping around, basking in the warmth of the instinct that told her that a song was about to be born. It wasn't long before the magnetism of the chorus Bill was singing drew me from the kitchen to the piano, and we finished the song that was to feed us better than any other food could have fed us:

I'm so glad I'm a part of the Family of God!
I've been washed in the fountain, cleansed by His blood.
Joint heirs with Jesus as we travel this sod,
For I'm part of the Family, the Family of God.

You will notice we say brother and sister 'round here,
It's because we're a Family and these folks are so near.
When one has a heartache we all share the tears,
And rejoice in each victory in this Family so dear.

From the door of an orphanage to the house of the King,
No longer an outcast, a new song I sing.
From rags unto riches, from the weak to the strong,
I'm not worthy to be here, but praise God I belong!

Since that Easter Sunday there have been heartaches
and victories in our own lives that have been shared by
the Family of God. It's been wonderful! In a world where
everything has to be paid for or earned in some tangible
way, where everybody seems to have an angle or an ulterior motive, there is no joy like the joy of knowing that we
are part of a Family that loves us and cares about us, no
matter what. They see our faults; they know our weaknesses. And they just love us anyway. Sometimes we do
dumb things and fall far short of our best hopes for ourselves, but the Family of God is always there to draw us
up to higher, more worthy goals, while always supporting
and undergirding us with their prayer and concern. In it
we all know that the Family is there to help us produce
our best for His Highest.

Ron is a very healthy, robust basketball coach these
days. His life is a strong witness in our community to the
power and love of Christ. When he and Darlene sing in
their simple, childlike way, "I'm so glad I'm a part of the
Family of God . . ." it is a very special moment for Bill and
me. Since the day that song was written, their little Diane
has had very serious but successful open-heart surgery,
and I can't tell you what a lovely sight it is to see her
frolicking on the playground of the Alexandria Elementary School with the other children at recess.

Praise be to Jesus, the sweet Rose of Sharon,
Praise to the Christ, the Redeemer of men;
Praise to the King who is reigning forever,
The Hope of the ages, my Master and Friend.

V

Because He Lives . . .

His life is real and needs no other argument. It will stand in obvious contrast to all replicas; it will draw anyone who is honestly searching for the Real Thing.

Come See Me

During the first miles of my journey, like most baby Christians, I wanted to run right out and convert the world. I guess I figured that all I had to do was say, "I did this and you should, too," and the world would stand in line to believe. It wasn't long before I was spiritually black-and-blue from running into blank walls—and very discouraged. I couldn't figure it out. I could plainly see that people were miserable and needed what I had found. And I had my testimony all whipped into shape for instant sharing. Yet there seemed to be a translation problem. Somehow, what I was saying so clearly (*I* thought) was not being understood. It was as if I were speaking in English but it was coming out in Swahili.

And it seemed that the more intelligent people were, the more educated, the more sophisticated, the harder it was for them to understand. They had a thousand questions that had to be resolved first. They had doubts and hang-ups to be worked out. They wanted to be sure it was all rational and sane and logical and safe. They wanted to fit it into neat philosophical schools of thoughts. They threw out terms like "mysticism" and "irrationalism" and "idealism."

I felt compassion for my troubled friends, for I, too, had asked the very same questions not so long before. I had studied the schools of thought and knew the terms. I wanted so much not to be guilty of dealing with their questions in the way that a few Christians had dealt with mine: to rigidly say, "Don't ask that!" or, "You should quit reading all those books and stick with the Word." I felt sure that the God of order who had created the perfect synchronizations of the universe and who had given people the brains to solve many of its complexities, would not say to a bright young seeker, "Don't ask that!"

But I found that just telling people what they ought to do was not the way. I know now, looking back, that the gentle Holy Spirit was trying to teach me that I had to really put my life on the line—not just my mouth. I had to learn to relax in Him and dare to trust. The sense of urgency I felt had been misdirected. It came out pushy and obnoxious.

One night our family was sitting in the middle of Suzanne's bed, having worship. Bill was reading some verses from John. We must have read them often before, but this time, because life was teaching me a lesson, my ears were really hearing. One of the disciples was feeling the same sense of excitement I felt. He had walked with Jesus, seen the miracles, felt the touch of Love's transforming power in his own life. He was in a hurry for *all* to know. If they could just see Jesus as he had seen Him, the whole world would be instantly convinced. So the disciple asked, ". . . Sir, why are you going to reveal yourself only to us disciples and not to the world at large?" (John 14:22 LB). Can't you just hear his mind working? "You need a good promoter. If we could just get this show on the road and get Your miracles before the masses, everyone could be converted!"

Even Jesus' rebuke was gentle. How like Him! He knew what redemption was going to cost. He would be before the masses, all right. On a cross.

> Jesus replied, "Because I will only reveal myself to those who love me and obey me. The Father will love them too, and we will come to them and live with

them. Anyone who doesn't obey me doesn't love me.
And remember, I'm not making up this answer to your
question! It is the answer given by the Father who sent
me."

John 14:23, 24 LB

So that was it. The world would have to come, not *en
masse,* but one at a time, because they dared to take the
risk of believing. Why had the truth of that eluded me?
Risk first—revelation after. Believe first—sight later. I had
had to come that way. All the questions in the world did
not bring the simple joy of knowing Jesus. It was all right
to ask them. But my mind never did figure out the answers by itself. I had to risk. Risk making a fool of myself.
Risk my rational mind on an irrational choice. And then
the answers had come. The pieces of the puzzle had fallen
into beautiful, logical place for me.

I couldn't *make* anyone believe. No words could explain it. No logic could convince the heart that would not
risk. What then? I would have to put my life on the line.
I would have to abandon all restraint, reserving nothing
back to be *His* person. *The being.* That was the secret.
Not doing or telling or acting, but being—*being God's
person*—gently, lovingly, constantly being Jesus where
I was.

This way was not going to be so simple and speedy as
I had hoped, nor so easy. It meant more than sitting
around philosophizing about it, even "witnessing." It
meant "living out" the proof as it had been lived out for
me.

The sense of urgency would remain, and often I have
prayed that the world would see enough Jesus in enough
people to give it the courage to take the risk of believing
—and do it in time!

But I couldn't cover the territory for the people I loved.

I couldn't take the risk for them. I could only share what had happened to me, not so much with my mouth as with my moments and days. And when the Holy Spirit had brought them to the place of risk, I could be available— just *be there* to sort of act as midwife for the birth. They would need someone then. Someone that had loved them and cared about them and prayed for them. I would be there. I couldn't push them or strong-arm them or harass them—even for their own good. But I could live with them and love them. I could laugh with them and cry with them and share their load, and when they were ready, I would be there!

> When you're ready to meet Jesus—
>> Come see me—
>> Come see me!
> When you're sick of sin and longing
>> to be free,
>> to be free.
> When you need a love that's gone much deeper
>> than your deepest sin—
> When you're ready to come home again,
>> no matter where you've been.
> When you're ready to meet Jesus
>> Come see me—
>> Come see me!

> I can't tell what's deep inside
>> earth's caverns—
> I've only read about their jewels
>> rich and rare.
> I've not explored the depths
>> of any ocean—
> But when you want to meet the Savior
>> I've been *there*.

> I've not walked or talked with earth's
>   most famous statesmen—
> Chances that I'll ever meet them
>   all are dim—
> But if you'd like to know
>   this King of Glory,
> I can take you to meet Jesus,
>   I know Him.

You know, there's been a wonderful freedom in finding out that the wooing of a soul is the Holy Spirit's business, *not mine.* I just had to be available to be His person. Now I know that I don't have to know everything about everything. I just need to know the one thing that matters in all of life: that Jesus Christ is a permanent resident in my heart and that He is available to anyone who longs to know Him. I just need to be on twenty-four-hour call to aid in the delivery.

> I Jesus have sent mine angel to testify unto you these things in the churches. I am the root and the offspring of David, and the bright and morning star.
> And the Spirit and the bride say, Come. And let him that heareth say, Come. And let him that is athirst come. And whosoever will, let him take the water of life freely.

> Revelation 22:16, 17

> Let him who is thirsty come to clear water,
> Let him who is hungry come by and eat;
> For money can't buy this cool living water,
> Or this milk and honey so sweet.

Lift Up Jesus

When we look at all the philosophical theories that beckon the minds of people today, we could get dizzy just thinking about them. Zen and Buddha, Hare Krishna and the Moonies, "mind dynamics" and "est," psychocybernetics and transcendental meditation, Satanism and the occult, and hundreds more raise voices in boisterous bedlam, vying for dominion of the mind. The soul of man is, as never before, under siege. Frighteningly enough, that includes the vulnerable minds and souls of the young, our own children—yours and ours.

The influences of dozens of these philosophies have seeped their way into textbooks, guidance counseling, television programing, movies, magazines, the daily newspaper, and even some schools of theology. What chance do the claims of Jesus Christ have in such an arena? How can the voice of the Master be heard above the din?

Depressing as all this may seem, we truly believe that now, more than ever before, the child of God has reason for excitement and confidence. We believe that the reason so many cults and philosophies have sprung up like mushrooms after a rain is that *now, more than ever before,* people are hungry for something real. They are searching, questing, longing to find the key to the formula of life. "What's It All About, Alfie?" is more than just a song. It's the cry for help of a sick generation.

People are tired of the clichés of materialism. All the phony promises of accumulated wealth, status, and influence have betrayed the inner longings of the human heart. So man has become a nomad, but it is not so much his feet that wander from place to place in search of fertile soil and better lands; it is his mind. Again and again he sets up camp in the promised land of some new theory and begins the adventure of spying out the land. But no matter how wild the claims or how attractive the promises, the soul of man will never find a place to rest until he finds the Real Thing, the Source of Life Abundant. He may find philosophical amusements and diversions to occupy his attention for a while, but sooner or later the basic needs of thirst and hunger for the Real Thing will drive him on.

Can the promise of Abundant Life in Jesus Christ be heard above the confusion? Is there any hope of the questing wanderer stumbling onto the claims of the Gospel?

If the Gospel of Christ were only a theology, an alternative among many philosophies, the prospects would be pretty dismal. Christianity would be merely making a bid in the marketplace of the mind for its measly share of disciples. But comparing the Good News of the Gospel to the philosophies of this world would be like comparing the rich and succulent fruit of a citrus tree to the dime-store waxen replicas.

It is with joy and confidence that we can take our message into the chaos of this world. There may be hundreds —even thousands—of voices, but it is the Real Thing for which man yearns. There is only one real Source who can fill the God-shaped vacuum in the human heart. There is only one Master who can transform a life, quench the thirst, satisfy the gnawing hunger, and fill the emptiness in the universe of the soul. It doesn't matter how many voices may be calling out pseudo-answers. When the honest heart hears the certain sound of the Real Thing, it will listen. The Gospel of Jesus Christ is not one of the answers, it is *the* answer. It is not a silly slogan painted on one of the placards of this world, bobbing up and down amid a sea of other billboards on the caucus floor. It is *the* banner flying high above the chaos. It has bought in blood its right to demand the attention of every man, woman, and child of Adam's race.

Jesus Himself said, "And I, if I be lifted up from the earth, will draw all men unto me" (John 12:32).

What a promise! No need for pessimism here. No call for fear or discouragement! The anticipation of the prospects of taking such a promise seriously leaves us tingling with excitement. The requirements of the promise are simple. Jesus doesn't demand that we out-talk, out-shout, out-think, or out-argue the philosophies of this world. He only says, "Just lift Me up; I'll draw all men unto Me." No competition here. Just lift up Jesus. Point to Jesus. Live like Jesus. Think and act and react like Jesus. That will get their attention. That sort of thinking and behavior is foreign to this world—loving with no strings attached; giving with no expectation of return; serving without ulterior motives; living with honesty and integrity even when no one is looking; living a code of morals that is neither dictated nor eroded by whims of society. Being Jesus where we are. Lifting up Him. "That's all it will take," He promises.

But if the attention of the milling masses is to be turned toward Jesus, we who bear His name must lift Him up. If the world is to find the Real Thing, we whose wandering souls have found our home in Him must be real. Perhaps the reason the lost take so long to sort out the truth is that the contrast between the "real" and the counterfeit has lost its cutting edge. Sometimes there just isn't enough "real" to go around. Sometimes we who bear His name allow ourselves to be distracted by the gimmicks of the other philosophies. We begin to wrap our certain statements in obscurities and theories.

I just looked up that word *theory* in the dictionary. It said: ". . . that branch of an art or science consisting of a knowledge of its *principles and methods* rather than its *practice.*" I guess that's what I mean. Too often we let the confused world trick us into formulating arguments about our principles and methods rather than saving our energy for *being* examples of the Real Thing. The validity of the Gospel of Christ is best stated in valid living rather than noisy argument. It is the contrast of the Abundant Life in Jesus that lifts Him up, that draws the questing heart.

There is a term used in the Bible that expresses this—*singleness of mind.* It means having a one-track mind about something that really matters. When I was a little girl, my grandpa used to plow the garden plot and corn patch with a plow pulled by a horse. I used to watch him harness the horse and hitch him to the plow. He'd let me walk along beside him as he turned the clods of dark Michigan soil, and sometimes I'd take an empty Campbell's Pork & Beans can to pick up fishing worms along the furrows. One time I remember asking Grandpa why he put those round leather things beside the horse's eyes. "Those are blinders," he told me. "They're called that because they blind the horse to everything except the job he has to do. Without them, he'd be distracted by things, and every time he looked away, there'd be a crooked place in the furrow. If he keeps his eyes straight ahead, the furrow will be straight."

Now, that's singleness of mind. And I think we, as serious disciples of our Lord, need to be single-minded about one thing: lifting up Jesus. We have to be real, through and through. If we are, the world will notice.

In front of our house there is a creek (pronounced, in Indiana, "crick") which feeds a small pond. That pond has become the haven for many forms of wildlife which have in turn become a source of joy for us and the children. Over the years, we have accumulated quite a population of wild and migratory birds (which no longer migrate because we feed them); various and sundry domesticated fowl (the Easter duck of every kid in town); a few misplaced water snakes; a pond full of crappies, catfish, blue-gills, and carp; a few soft-shelled turtles (who unfortunately feed on baby ducklings); and, from April to August, a large community of purple martins and bank swallows (who conspire to keep at a comfortable minimum the mosquito population that would otherwise threaten the pleasure of family picnics and fishing). Somehow in the process of time we also acquired a pair of white farm geese, who in turn raised a gosling. The three of them float up and down the creek, looking very regal in comparison to the mud hens and brown mallards that share their habitat. Often strangers both to us and to this fowl world have stopped to admire our "swans."

Last summer we became acquainted with a farmer not so far away who raises many kinds of wild and domesticated waterfowl. My mother and I took the children and drove over to see what he had. There were pintails and wood ducks and peafowls. There were breeds of wild geese we'd never seen before. And there were swans. He agreed to sell us a pair of them. What a time we had bringing two full-grown swans home in a big cardboard box in the back end of my tiny Monza. There were mother and I in the front seat, three children in the backseat (which has two bucket seats with an island dividing them), and two huge birds with necks like elephant trunks in a box in the back. We managed to tie the hatchback door over the open box top so as to partially hold the birds in, but their necks kept darting out and around the open edge toward the backseat. It was an interesting trip home, to say the least.

When we got there, the swans were delighted with their new home. They whistled and splashed and scooped water in their cupped wings to throw over their heads. They dove to the bottom with their long necks, then stretched high in the air and flapped their wings. They frolicked like children on the first day of spring. But by evening they had settled down to map out the territory that would be their turf (or water rights) and were happily "at home." What a sight they were, gliding with grace and majesty across the sun's crimson reflection in the water, their regal heads held high above the elegant arch of their necks.

That was nearly a year ago. In all that time not one person has referred to our farm geese as "swans." To even the novice, they seem like mundane creatures plodding along, dwarfed in size and suddenly awkward beside the glorious, lovely grace of the real item!

The transforming power of the Gospel of Jesus Christ does not need our arguments. It is its own proclamation. It only needs to be revealed to the world in the lives and words and attitudes of those who have been transformed and reclaimed by it. We only need to *be* the Real Thing. The world isn't longing for another philosophy to add to the already maddening maze of things. It doesn't need a new high or a new theory. It is dying for want of *life*— His LIFE. Let's listen with compassion beyond the noise of words to the real cry of man's heart:

> I'm not trying to find
> Just some new frame of mind
> That will change my old point of view;
> For I've been through them all—
> Deep inside, nothing's changed, nothing's new.
> I'm not seeking a gift
> Or emotional lift—
> But the one thing I'm longing to do
> Is to lift up my cup
> And let You fill it up
> With just You.
>
> I have searched all around
> In the husks that abound

But I find no nourishment there;
Now my strength's almost gone
And I feel the pull of despair—
Yet my thirst drives me on
And I stumble along
Over ground so barren and dry . . .
There's a Spring just ahead—LIVING WATER!
"Lord, fill me!" I cry.

More of You!
More of You!
I've had all but what I need,
Just more of You!
Of things I've had my fill,
And yet I hunger still.
Empty and bare,
Lord, hear my prayer
For more of YOU!

For the scripture says, "I will destroy the wisdom of the wise, I will set aside the understanding of the scholars." So then, where does that leave the wise men? Or the scholars? Or the skillful debaters of this world? God has shown that this world's wisdom is foolishness! . . .

But God has brought you into union with Christ Jesus, and God has made Christ to be our wisdom; by him we are put right with God, we become God's own people, and are set free. Therefore, as the scripture says, "Whoever wants to boast must boast of what the Lord has done."

1 Corinthians 1:19, 20, 30, 31 TEV

These are exciting times. People are searching. They are looking for real meaning in their lives. They have tried the superficial; now—more than ever before—people are looking for something more. What a marvelous

time to lift up Jesus! For the Gospel of our Lord is not a
mere philosophy in competition to the avalanche of
philosophies that vie for man's allegiance. He is LIFE itself.
Let's lift Him up, for He has promised that any one of us
who claims His name is a majority when the Holy Spirit
is with him. What we live and proclaim is LIFE—the Real
Thing!

> Why art thou cast down, O my soul? and why art
> thou disquieted within me? *Hope thou in God:* for I
> shall praise him who is the health of my countenance
> and my God.
>
> Psalms 42:5

Oh, lift up Jesus!
Just lift up Jesus!
He's the only One can fill the void in me.
Just lift up Jesus!
Lift up Jesus!
He's the only One we really need to see!

Listen to their voices. They want the Real Thing:

Oh, I had most everything
That affluent life could bring—
I'd do anything to conquer and succeed;
Yet the more I won the game,
The more empty I became,
'Til He touched me at my very point of need.

Listen to the young. They want something more:

It is circus time inside
I could go on every ride
And be dazzled by how bright the lights can be.
But I know the thrills will fade,
Life is more than a parade,
I need something lasting—Lift up Christ for me!

They don't all cry in English:

Hear the voice from far away:
"We are dying while you play—
We are bound by chains from which we would be free.
We have seen your wealth and goods
But we long for better *food;*
Sir, your Jesus is the One we need to see."

Hear the prayer of young parents:

In our homes we would be wise
When we look in children's eyes—
How we long to make some memories they'll hold dear.
Won't you wrap us in Your love?
Make us "harmless as a dove"?
Oh, Lord, stay with us—and make Your home right here!

Oh, lift up Jesus!
Just lift up Jesus!
He's the only One can fill the void in me.
Lift up Jesus!
Lift up Jesus!
He's the only One we really need to see.

Between the Cross and Heaven

Someone has described the college years as the span between adolescence and adulthood, when we are neither accountable to nor responsible for anyone else—during which we are afforded the luxury of four years to study theories in a theoretical community under professors who make their living in a world of theory. Education is what we have left after we've forgotten all we've learned. There may be some hint of truth to all that.

By the same token, in the realm of the Spirit, perhaps the "life in Christ" means those things of permanent value that have come to possess us after we've learned and put in our back pocket all the theological concepts and then gone on with the business of living. In other words, knowing about *Creation* and *Reincarnation* and *Redemption* and *Substitution* and *Ascension* and the *Trinity* and the *Indwelling* and the *Second Coming* means little except inasmuch as the truth of them comes to possess men and women at the level of daily life and in some dramatic way alters a person's choices, values, and life-style.

Sometimes it's fun for us believers to entertain ourselves in our cozy "in circle" of the church world by discussing and verbalizing to each other the various points of theology. I must confess there are few things I enjoy more than a good theological discussion with people who have sharp minds and healthy egos, people who are able to disagree without feeling (or making me feel) threatened. But while this is great entertainment, I'll just have to admit it does little to convince the world that Christ is the answer to the gut-level problems of their lives. We throw around and argue over terms like Calvinism, Arminianism, eternal security, the second blessing, and the charismatic demonstration, and can often give very impressive discourses on why our particular persuasion is The Way, quoting literally yards of Scripture to support our stance. But while we are writing our theses and compiling our creeds, the bewildered world is scratching its head, wondering what all that has to do with the problems of a drug-addicted son or an unmarried pregnant daughter or a marriage that is "daily hell" or a job that is unbearably meaningless. Many times I have sat in revival services and listened to evangelists and singers tell folks how dedicated they are to have been away from home for ten weeks straight, and I've seen the blank expression on the face of some "regular guy" in the pew and have wondered if he wouldn't rather know whether these servants of God ever take out the garbage or mow their own yards.

When we do make an effort to turn our attention to the world, to be "evangelical" (which means sharing our story), it seems that we tend to get hung up on two points of theology: "getting saved" and "going to heaven." More songs are written, more sermons preached, more tracts and literature are printed on those two themes than on any other topics in the religious world. A good share of the communication with the "lost" tells the story of how bad we were before, how exciting the moment of encounter, and how that encounter caused us to turn around and head for heaven. Most of the rest of it describes, in glowing terms, the place somewhere in the blue beyond— where we will walk on golden streets through gates of pearl and sit for unlimited eternities doing absolutely nothing but resting "as ceaseless ages roll."

Now I may be weird, but an eternal reward like that would never attract and persuade me to leave a life of sin

and begin that to-the-death struggle with the enemy
which is required to break binding habits, forge new
friendships, leave old life-styles, and begin a new way of
living. I love green meadows and sea breezes and cool
forests and dangling my feet in a brook too much to want
to trade that for cold streets of gold. I love people and
relationships and learning and hard work and growth too
much to be attracted by a "reward" that would force me
into premature and permanent retirement and waste
forever all the discoveries this life only intimates but
never has time to fully reveal.

Please don't distort my intentions. We couldn't believe
more in salvation or in heaven. But the moment of accepting Jesus as Lord is different for everyone and what comes
after that moment is what this journey is all about.

Earlier in the book I gave you my personal testimony.
It is a truthful and (I'm afraid as I read back over it) an
emotional account of a crisis moment in my life. But that
is exactly what it was, a crisis *moment.* Granted, it was a
special and very sacred moment for me, but only one
moment. There have been countless other meaningful
moments on my journey since I chose to travel with the
Lord. I am convinced there will be hundreds more if I live
long enough and continue to grow. But I would much
prefer that you judge the validity of my commitment to
the Lord Jesus by the growth and consistency of my daily
life than by how spectacular is my story of the conversion
moment.

It saddens me that we have put such a premium on a
Christian's *testimony,* meaning his story of conversion,
and that some regular, church-type, dull testimonies have
had to be "spruced up and juiced up" a little to be accepted as real in the inner circles, while all too little attention is paid to the other words of Jesus, besides "You must
be born again."

We have put such an unrealistic burden of expectation

on the new convert. We all want to tell him how he's
going to feel and react when he comes to the Lord. We
want him to sigh or cry or leap to his feet or shout or pout
or shake about like the corporate "we" did. And if he
happens to be the quiet, determined, scientific type who
simply and quietly determines in his heart to make Jesus
the Lord and Master of his life starting now, we turn up
our sanctimonious noses and whisper behind our hands at
the missionary circle that we really doubt whether he
ever "prayed through."

I hesitate to say this, but the words of Jesus tend to
suggest that the "proof of the pudding" can be seen on
Monday morning in the attitudes he displays, the choices
and value judgments he makes, and the way he aligns his
priorities. And, I might add, the *same* criteria tend to be
used to pass judgment on the rest of us, too. To tell you
the truth, I believe the world is a little weary of altar
services that don't alter lives.

When I was a kid, I used to love Wednesday-night
prayer meeting. The reason was not so much the spiritual
blessing I received while attending, as the fact that it was
"the best show in town." We were too poor to have a TV,
we weren't allowed to go to movies, and we didn't dance;
so the next best option for entertainment in my young life
was to listen to the vivid descriptions of the life of sin and
degradation that some of the church folks had been saved
from. Many of those before-and-after stories dwelled
longer and with quite some relish on the "before." It
occurred to me in those days that it must be very difficult
for God to keep our sins buried in the deepest of the sea
when we insist on deep-sea diving again and again. And
it seemed that in some cases the stories of the forgotten
past grew more colorful as time went by. This set quite a
precedent for the young and innocent to live up to. Although it was never affirmed aloud, we generally got the
impression from the chorus of *Amens* that followed the

stories of the worst pasts that if we wanted people to take our conversions seriously, we had better do some things that we could get saved *from.*

As it turned out, I never did do anything that would make a good story, and to this day I hesitate to tell about my conversion. People always seem so disappointed that there isn't more to it. It isn't very exciting to hear about a kid who grew up in the church, saw both saints and hypocrites, watched closely the consistencies and inconsistencies, asked a lot of uncomfortable questions, struggled with doubts and conflicts, and chose to risk everything to be God's person. Even the misery of my search was mostly *internal,* so the story is really quite dull. Bill's story is quite similar.

Lately, God has been teaching us some things about this, and we have come to see that some of the most violent changes in a person's behavior may very well come in the hidden, sneaky little areas like attitudes and internal reactions. Some of the greatest upheavals in a life can come when the Holy Spirit begins to lay His finger on our resentments and hidden animosities, our motives and ulterior intentions, our uncommitted dreams and ambitions, our not-so-obvious failures and shortcuts.

We have begun to learn that it is not nearly so important that we be able to glibly recite the "day and the hour" as it is to know that our business dealings are above reproach, our motives are clear, and our attitudes toward the Lord and other people are healthy. We have begun to discover that taking care of our bills on time, not asking for favors from the world because we are Christians, giving an honest day's work, and being absolutely dependable in following through on assignments are sometimes a more certain "witness" to the life-changing power of redemption than reciting the "plan of salvation" from memory or praying in church on Sunday—no matter how good these may be. The Holy Spirit has been teaching us that it doesn't matter how many people notice that we bow our heads or hear us return thanks in a restaurant, if we still treat the waitress like our personal Slave for a Day and leave a chintzy tip.

Jesus spent a lot of time talking about getting to the root of the problem. He said, "Let's not talk about adultery; let's talk about lust." He said that there's no reason to worry about stealing if we can't conquer the nasty problem of covetousness. He said, "Let's not theorize over how we're going to punish killers; let's do something about hatred." He said, "Why waste all this time talking about just what kind of oath is 'swearing' and what kind is not!" He made it simple. Don't swear. *Period.* If you want to say *yes,* say *yes* and mean it. If you want to say *no,* say *no* and let the honor of your word be enough. He said, "Don't spend any time at all thinking up ways to get even. You won't need them if you're going to be My person, because My way is the way of the second mile, doing *more* than is expected of you, forgiving even if you have been the one wronged." Jesus told us not to worry about parceling out our love and friendship to those who have earned it. Loving your friends and those most lovable is no big deal! Anybody can do that. "But I say unto you, Love your *enemies,* bless them *that curse you,* pray for them *which despitefully use you,* and persecute you" (Matthew 5:44).

There are some lines from a song that is in the first chapter, but I'd like to quote another section here, because it has to do with the things we've been learning from the words of Jesus about getting to the basic problem:

> Don't want to cast my vote
> For men who only promise programs
> Just assuring the affluence I have known.

May I see the *real poverty,*
The kind that only God can see,
And know that "men can't live by bread alone."

Don't want to spend my time
Just putting Band-Aids on the patient
Who is eaten up with cancer from within.
When we have the news that "Jesus saves!"
And raises dead men from their graves
With water where they'll never thirst again!

In our duties as citizens, in our daily jobs, in our involve-
ments in community affairs, in our dealings with our
neighbors, in our reactions to those nasty people who are
difficult to love, the Lordship of Christ in our lives must
make a difference. There's a whole lot in the words of
Jesus between "Ye must be born again" and "Lo, I come
quickly," things that sometimes would be easier to ignore.
But if our driving passion is to really know God in His
fullest, these are words that must be reckoned with. And
if we're serious about this business of discipleship, the
claims of Christ will demand so much of our energies—
and the excitement of the adventure of "becoming" will
be so exhilarating—that we will have little time or appetite for mulling over the husks of the past.

There is a very exciting book we've been reading lately,
called *Knowing God* by J. I. Packer, and I'd like to quote
a bit from this very painful but glorious book. Speaking of
the forgiven experiences of our past he says:

> Constantly we find ourselves slipping into bitterness
> and apathy and gloom as we reflect on them, which we
> frequently do. The attitude we show to the world is a
> sort of dried-up stoicism, miles removed from the 'joy
> unspeakable and full of glory' which Peter took for

granted that his readers were displaying (I Peter 1:8). 'Poor souls,' our friends say of us, 'how they've *suffered*' —and that is just what we feel about ourselves! But these private mock heroics have no place at all in the minds of those who really know God. They never brood on might-have-beens; they never think of the things they have missed, only on what they have gained. 'What things were gain to me, these have I counted loss for Christ,' wrote Paul. 'Yea verily, and I count all things to be loss for the excellency of the knowledge of Christ Jesus my Lord: for whom I suffered the loss of all things, and do count them but dung, that I may gain Christ and be found in him . . . that I may know him . . .' (Philippians 3:7–10). When Paul says he counts the things he lost 'dung', he means not merely that he does not think of them as having any value, but also that he does not live with them constantly in his mind: what normal person spends his time nostalgically dreaming of manure? Yet this, in effect, is what many of us do. It shows how little we have in the way of true knowledge of God.

There is no stronger evidence to the person on the outside looking in than a valid personal testimony. But what that person really needs to hear is not some morbid description of an ancient experience, but what the love of Jesus is doing in our lives now, this morning, yesterday. The initial moment may be a place to begin—but has anything happened since then?

Let us suppose that you and I share the acquaintance of a man about thirty years old. We work with him, we see him around town, his kids go to school with our kids. Whenever we meet this man, no matter what the headlines of the newspaper, the state of the economy, or what season or holiday is current, the man has one topic of conversation and it begins something like this:

"Well, how are you today? Let me tell you what once happened to me. It was about four A.M. when my mother first began to have pains in her back. At first they were very slight but gradually they became more severe and woke her from a deep sleep. She in turn awakened my father and he rushed her to the hospital. They thought that she was nearly ready to deliver, but due to some complications [which he goes on to describe in some detail], the labor was long and difficult. Finally, about noon the next day, I began to be thrust out into the world. It was frightening and quite a shock to leave the warm womb and be pushed into the cold world. At first I cried my little heart out, but soon I was cleaned with warm water and wrapped in a soft blanket. My mother held me close and I began to realize how good it was to be alive. Oh, it was wonderful—sunshine pouring into the room, a bouquet of fresh yellow daisies on the windowsill, a feeling of knowing that I was loved and cared for. Oh, I wish I could tell you how exciting it all was!"

Now, no one would doubt the validity of that story. Obviously, the man had been born. He's telling us the truth. But we would consider the telling and retelling of that story a little abnormal behavior for a full-grown man. Surely, something funny or exciting or sad or fulfilling has happened to him since, which he could tell us about.

In the physical world we would consider that behavior somewhat strange, but in the spiritual world—in matters of eternal importance—we sometimes consider similar behavior perfectly normal. But I'm afraid that the world, after once hearing the story of our spiritual birth, would like to ask, "What has life been like since you were re-born? Do you love your wife and kids more? Has this experience affected your work? Do you panic and get uptight and lose your temper like you used to? Since Calvary—what?" Somewhere between the past blessing and the promised reward there's a whole lot of living going on! Does the invitation of Jesus to "follow Me" speak to those days in between? Can Jesus give meaning to the monotony of a job? Will the Abundant Life in Christ help us not to scream at each other when we get home? Does Christianity speak to the frustrations and stress that tie a stomach in knots and give birth to ulcers and high blood pressure? Will it change our attitudes on the freeway, when traffic is bumper-to-bumper and some guy crowds in front and puts a dent in our car? I mean: Between the cross and heaven, does serving Jesus make sense?

Jesus said, *Come unto me all ye who labour and are heavy laden and I will give you rest. Take my yoke upon you . . .* (Matthew 11:28, 29). [Can you fathom the implications of this invitation? Sharing the harness of life with Jesus Himself, having at our disposal all the strength and muscle of God to pull our load, do our work, meet the demands of our day?] *Take my yoke upon you, and learn of me; for I am meek and lowly in heart:* [He's not going to shout at us when we fail or are weak or discouraged—just love and encourage and lift and pull] *and ye shall find rest unto your souls* (v. 29). [Imagine what He is promising! Rest on the inside, a way to "cool it" when everything is in turmoil on the outside, contentment in the eye of the storm.]

Yes, Virginia, the Abundant Life *does* have something to do with life. And if you can imagine, you get all that and heaven, too. *But* between the cross and heaven there's a whole lot of living going on—and we mean *living!*

> Oh, the joy I felt when I met the Saviour's
>   worth sharing,
> And it's so exciting just to think of the
>   place He's preparing—
> But most of what the Lord had to say
> Says He *cares* about what I'm doing today;
> And life is more than just an interlude
> Between the first verse and the last!

Between the cross and heaven
There's a whole lot of living going on.
When we meet the Saviour then our new
    life is only begun.
There's caring and lifting and there's loving to do.
There's happiness in singing the song!
Between the cross and heaven
There's a whole lot of living going on!

Now, having said all that, I think we'll still go on
sharing the story of how Jesus came to possess our
lives. And you share your story, too. Nothing is more
powerful or more indisputable than a person saying, "I
only know it happened to me." But let's tell about
more than the moment of birth. Let's include the current things God is doing in our lives. Then let's back
up our story with valid living, being very sure that
we're not getting vicarious thrills out of recounting the
"life of sin." As Paul suggests, that's not sharing a witness; that's dwelling on the "dung," and there's nothing healthy about that.

In short, we want to just grow up in the good things of
the Lord. We want to be weaned and then nourished with
the solid food God has for us. We long to stand strong and
tall and healthy, to grow beyond diapers and formula and
tantrums.

Paul wrote to the Corinthians:

    . . . I could not talk to you as I talk to men who have
    the Spirit; I had to talk to you as men of this world, as
    children in the Christian faith. I had to feed you milk,
    not solid food, because you were not ready for it. And
    even now you are not ready for it, because you still live
    as men of this world. When there is jealousy among
    you, and you quarrel with one another, doesn't this

prove that you are men of this world, living by this
world's standards?

I Corinthians 3:1–3 TEV

My daddy was a preacher. I remember so well the times
when he'd answer the phone and then hang up, looking
discouraged and weary. He would pick up his coat and his
Bible, and I'd say, "Where are you going, Daddy?" He'd
look down at me, shake his head as if there was something
he wanted to say that I couldn't quite yet understand, and
he'd reply, "To take them the bottle, Shug. To take them
the bottle." I didn't know what he meant then, but I do
now. He was going to nurse along some Christian who
refused to grow up, who was never strong enough to be
weaned, who had to be coddled and babied along, year
after weary year. And the sad thing was not so much how
tired Daddy got of running a nursery for spiritual tod-
dlers, but that, for many of these people, their refusal to
grow up in Jesus stunted their natural maturation process
and made dwarfs and cripples of them. And they never
knew the joy of their salvation or the things which belonged to their peace.

Oh, God has so many good things for us! We don't want
to settle for baby food and feasting on the miseries of the
past. How we long to grow and reach and learn and experience all He has for us! And how we pray for the good
Abundant Life in Him for you! Let's not settle for less. No
wonder Paul prayed for those he loved in Ephesus:

. . . that Christ will be more and more at home in
your hearts, living within you as you trust in him. May
your roots go down deep into the soil of God's marvelous love; and may you be able to feel and understand,
as all God's children should, how long, how wide, how
deep, and how high his love really is; and to experience

this love for yourselves. . . . so at last you will be filled
up with God himself.

Ephesians 3:17–19 LB

I Could Never Outlove the Lord

There's a story that our children love, and we read it
often at our house. I hesitate to recommend it, because I
know how much some people hate it when a friend is
always telling them what they ought to read. But even if
you are a grown-up—even if you hate to read and have no
children to tease you into doing it anyway—I think I'll risk
it and tell you that this is a pretty special story.

It's called *The Velveteen Rabbit,* and it was written by
a lady named Margery Williams, whom I've never met
but certainly would like to someday. The story is about a
little Rabbit made of velveteen who made his way into a
little boy's stocking one year at Christmas. At first the boy
noticed him, but it wasn't long, with all the excitement of
the festivities and other more spectacular gifts, before the
little stuffed Rabbit was tossed into a corner of the nursery
floor and forgotten. He was feeling very neglected indeed, and the only one who would even talk to him was
the Skin Horse.

"What is REAL?" asked the Rabbit one day, when
they were lying side by side near the nursery fender,
before Nana came to tidy the room. "Does it mean
having things that buzz inside you and a stick-out handle?"

"Real isn't how you are made," said the Skin Horse. "It's a thing that happens to you. When a child loves you for a long, long time, not just to play with, but REALLY loves you, then you become Real."

"Does it hurt?" asked the Rabbit.

"Sometimes," said the Skin Horse, for he was always truthful. "When you are Real you don't mind being hurt."

"Does it happen all at once, like being wound up," he asked, "or bit by bit?"

"It doesn't happen all at once," said the Skin Horse. "You become. It takes a long time. That's why it doesn't often happen to people who break easily, or have sharp edges, or who have to be carefully kept. Generally, by the time you are Real, most of your hair has been loved off, and your eyes drop out and you get loose in the joints and very shabby. But these things don't matter at all, because once you are Real you can't be ugly, except to people who don't understand."

The real. How this sick old world longs for it, gropes for it. How distorted is the Hollywood-and-Fifth-Avenue picture of "real" and "love" which we so often accept without question! How far it is from Hollywood to the "home-place of the heart"!

The other day Bill came to take me to lunch. The bakery was full, Hoadley's was closed, so we went to the White Spot. (When you live in a town the size of ours, it doesn't take you long to make a selection.) While we were waiting for our food, a teacher Bill had had in grade school came in with her husband. Bill had talked of her often—her love of learning, her energy and enthusiasm for teaching. It was she who had taught Bill to love grammar and had inspired him later to choose to teach it himself. But this day she came in very slowly, holding to her husband's arm. She had been stricken by a stroke some months before and had just recently been released from the hospital. There was such gentleness in the way her husband pulled out her chair and took her coat. The way he looked at her told us that there was something he was seeing that went beyond the face wearied and pale from long days of suffering. He reached across the table and tenderly untied her bandana, lovingly patting her cheek as he did so. He then unfolded her napkin and helped her to order. Everything about the way he looked at her and held her hand declared that she was his princess and he was her adoring knight.

The disinterested passerby might have seen only an elderly couple, past the prime of life by Hollywood standards, and certainly incapable of romance. But what does Hollywood know? There was something in the way these two people related to each other that made us know that somewhere—far back down the road—two lovers, perhaps then young and beautiful, had made a commitment to each other. Somewhere they had joined their hands before an altar and repeated those familiar words—"To love and to cherish, 'til death us do part." They had meant it. They had loved each other, invested in each other, and the two had "become one flesh." And as a result—their love had grown to be *real*. You're right, Skin Horse: "It doesn't happen all at once. . . . You become. It takes a long time."

Bill reached for my hand across the table. We bowed our heads silently. I knew he was praying, as I was: "Lord, make our love grow like that. Make our commitment to each other *real*. Let us always see each other through love's eyes."

Bill has an Aunt Lillie. She is eighty-four, and I wish you could know her. I suppose she's had more trouble and heartache in her lifetime than anyone we know, but what a spirit! Still alert and witty, she brightens the day of anyone who stops by her tiny apartment for tea. The children love her, for she is one of them. No generation gap there. (The "gap," it seems to me, is only between immediately succeeding generations, but when time and wisdom have brought us full circle, there is rarely a gap between the aged and the child.) They understand each other and seem to speak a sort of language of vibrations that transcend the awkwardness of archaic expressions and words now fallen into disuse.

Now I suppose if you saw Aunt Lillie, you would just see an elderly woman with gray hair and wrinkled skin and fading vision. But the other day Bill came in after having stopped up at Aunt Lillie's, and he said, "Aunt Lillie is such a pretty lady. She always has been pretty." Now, you might not understand that. Pretty. At eighty-four, pretty? But I do. The children do. The family does. She *is* pretty. Sparkling eyes. Mischievous grin. Long, graceful fingers. You might not see it right off. But love does. Bill sees it. I see it. The children notice. Aunt Lillie is beautiful, "always has been" and, I suspect, always will be. As the Skin Horse says, ". . . once you are Real," you can't become unreal again. It lasts for always. ". . . once you are Real you can't be ugly, except to people who don't understand."

My father died a couple of Christmases ago, and every evening since, my mother has joined our family for the evening meal. One evening when it was Benjy's turn to sit beside her, he stopped eating and looked up at her. He hesitantly reached up his little hand and stroked her velvet-soft cheek. Almost as if he were oblivious to the presence of the rest of us, momentarily secluded with his grandma in a tiny universe of their own, he said aloud, "Oh, Grandma, I love it when you come. You're beautiful!" Her response—though it lasted only a fleeting moment—is fixed in my memory like a frozen frame in a motion picture. Her eyes softened as he looked at her. Suddenly, she was once more a young model in a soft-pink picture hat, parading before the admiring eyes of the wholesale buyers at a dress show. She was the beloved of the young Lee Sickal, fresh from the farm. She was the hopeful young school teacher from Hannibal, Missouri. Love had worked its magic. The guileless adoration of a little boy had been the Real Thing, and the power of it had worked its instant miracle.

> "Real isn't how you are made," said the Skin Horse. "It's a thing that happens to you. When a child loves you for a long, long time, not just to play with, but REALLY loves you, then you become Real."
> "Does it hurt?" asked the Rabbit.
> "Sometimes," said the Skin Horse. . . .

Sometimes. . . .

There is nothing in the world that leaves one so open to attack, nothing that makes one so vulnerable, as *loving*. In fact, vulnerability is what love is all about: opening oneself to another, heart and all, nothing held back. One can get hurt that way. There's nothing safe about it. Love lays one wide open to hurts.

Many people these days choose not to take such a risk. This is the day of the noncommitment relationship. It seems as if most of the "now generation" is singing with Pinocchio, "I got no strings to hold me down, to make me laugh or make me frown; I am free and you can see, I got no strings on me!"

Songs and literature and art reinforce all this. About the nearest thing to an old-fashioned love song we can find these days is a plea to help us "make it through the night," while the tidal wave of pornographic photography and literature has reduced the physical body, the God-intended "temple of the Holy Spirit," to just so much flesh to be sold by the pound in the degenerate meat markets of the mind.

Parents who have seen their friends hurt by the way-

wardness of their children vow not to get so involved with
their own, and children hurt by the selfishness of the
do-your-own-thing philosophy of their parents make up
their minds to build protective walls around their emotions, so thick and high that no threatening communication can penetrate them.

We feel it everywhere. The hostility is in the air, on the
streets, in the schoolroom, in the community. "Don't get
too close. I don't want to trust you. I might get hurt." It's
on the faces of the children. It's in the eyes of the teenag-
ers. It's in the conversation at the beauty shop and the
laundromat. It's at the office and in the executive council
and in the factory: Protect yourself. Play it safe. Don't let
anyone rip you off. Keep your guard up. Don't get hurt.

In the midst of this uptight generation, Jesus calls us to
discipleship. "Love as I have loved you," He says. "Don't
just pretend that you love others: really love them . . ."
(Romans 12:9 LB).

The world says, "Do what you have to and no more."
Jesus says, "Do *more* than is demanded of you. If someone
wants you to walk with him a mile, walk two. If he wants
your coat, give him that and your shirt, too."

The world says, "Don't let 'em walk on you. Stand up
for your rights. Let 'em know how lucky they are to have
you." Jesus says, "Never pay back evil for evil. Do things
in such a way that everyone can see you are honest clear
through. Don't quarrel with anyone . . ." (Romans 12:17, 18
LB).

Over and over the Bible used the word *compassion*.
There has never been a time when it was more needed
than now. So many seem to be sealed into their little cages
of fear and apprehension. Paranoia is practically epi-
demic. Hurt and disillusioned with life, like frightened
animals they grasp tenaciously their pitiful holdings and,
in the process, squeeze the very life out of what they hold
so tightly. Hungry for affection and warmth, yet afraid to

risk the longtime investment of commitment, they fear
the risk of opening their hands and hearts to the real
fulfillment of inner longings.

It is to such a time as this that Jesus—the human expression of all the creative love of God—invites us to take the
risk of loving. He offers to share with us His cross—the
execution of the "safe way"—in exchange for the gift of
Real Life.

> Then said Jesus unto his disciples, If any man will
> come after me, let him deny himself, and take up his
> cross, and follow me. For whosoever will save his life
> shall lose it: and whosoever will lose his life for my sake
> shall find it.
>
> Matthew 16:24, 25

Only love can break the cycle of fear and suspicion.
How our world needs love that will take the risk of reaching out, touching hurts, breaking down walls of distrust.
Only simple Christlike love can invade the citadel of cyni-
cisms.

There is risk. Love will leave us vulnerable. But to
choose to be safe is to choose to die a little every day on
the inside—die to tenderness and sensitivity and hope—
die to the grand pleasures in simple things: the laughter
of children, the joy of the dawn, the deep rewards of
permanent relationships.

In a world that preaches a gospel of winning and getting ahead and playing it safe. Jesus invites us to let go, to
risk it all and dare to lose. He invites us to share His cross
as our entrance fee into a society where you have to lose
even to get in.

But in love there is power. Love can kill fear. Love can
tear down walls and build bridges. Love can transform
ugliness into beauty, trade cynicism for trust, and change

suspicion into faith. It is the presence of God's love in a human life that gives us the courage to believe. It is the seed of all hope. It is the enticement to trust, to risk, to try, to go on. It is the only true antidote for despondency and despair. It is, in short, what the Abundant Life is all about. Jesus made it possible to break the cycle of despair by invading our world with God's love—by taking love's risk.

I had won all I could win;
There was no place I hadn't been,
Yet my heart was just so needy and so poor.
Then I heard Him gently say:
"Lose it all—and find My Way."
So I gave it up
And found it all . . . and more!

I was frantic to survive;
I was racing to arrive,
And I walked on any standing in my way.
Then I watched my schemes all die
And I realized that I
Could find New Life
Because the "old" had died that day.

I lost it all to find *everything!*
I died a pauper
To be born a king.
When I learned how to lose
I found out how to win!
Oh! I lost it all
        TO FIND EVERYTHING!

Yes, Skin Horse, sometimes it hurts. It isn't easy to give up, take the risk, and choose death—so that we can live. There are times when loving hurts. There are times we'd rather just be a wind-up toy: mechanical, metallic, flashy, precut at the factory. Sometimes it is easier to just buzz across the floor at the direction of some mainspring we're not responsible for. But, you're right, Skin Horse, that may be easier; but those kinds of toys never know the magic difference which love makes. They never know the joy of becoming *real.* Becoming LOVE'S person is usually a painful process. But so is the struggle that brings the butterfly from its cocoon into the bright warm sunshine. So is the stretching that pushes the sprout out of its prison casing, through the stubborn sod and into the morning.

In friendships, in parenthood, in marriage, in family relationships, in neighboring, there is the risk of hurt. Friends can betray us, children may disappoint us. Husbands or wives may take more than they give. Parents may misunderstand our motives. Neighbors may refuse to be amiable. No matter. To love by freely giving is its own reward. To be possessed by LOVE and to in turn give LOVE away is to find the secret of Abundant Life. He who would really live must die. He who would really win must lose. He who would be *real* must accept the transforming miracle of LOVE'S redemption. Only then are we truly free to take the risk of loving others. The more we love, the more we are by LOVE possessed. It's as if our daring to love hollows out ever-widening spaces in our hearts into which His love can flow.

The reason we can dare to risk loving others is that "God has for Christ's sake loved us." Think of it! We are loved—eternally, totally, individually, unreservedly— loved! Nothing can take God's love away. We don't have to be afraid of losing it, offending it. We don't have to earn it. We only need to accept it. We are loved. By the One who knows us best. God knows everything there is to know about us—yet He loves us. If we are so loved, we can dare to like ourselves. We don't have to be defensive or self-protective or wary. No man can do us internal harm.

No rejection can discourage us. No betrayal can dishearten us. No assault can destroy us. We are loved!

And so God's ultimate risk of loving us with His own Son has broken the vicious chain of fear and distrust. He loves us! Once we have accepted His love and been made *real* —"new creatures in Christ Jesus," nothing can ever make us afraid to love again. We are loved! We are of value! We belong to God!

So there is now no condemnation awaiting those who belong to Christ Jesus. For the power of the life-giving Spirit—and this power is mine through Christ Jesus—has freed me from the vicious circle of sin and death. We aren't saved from sin's grasp by knowing the commandments of God, because we can't and don't keep them, but God put into effect a different plan to save us. He sent his own Son in a human body like ours —except that ours are sinful—and destroyed sin's control over us. . . . Who then can ever keep Christ's love from us? When we have trouble or calamity, when we are hunted down or destroyed, is it because he doesn't love us anymore? And if we are hungry, or penniless, or in danger, or threatened with death, has God deserted us?

Romans 8:1–3, 35 LB

No. . . . I am convinced that nothing can ever separate us from his love. Death can't, and life can't. The angels won't, and all the powers of hell itself cannot keep God's love away. Our fears for today, our worries about tomorrow, or where we are—high above the sky, or in the deepest ocean—*nothing will ever be able to separate us from the love of God demonstrated by our Lord Jesus Christ when he died for us* [italics added].

Romans 8:36–39 LB

We are loved! He took the first risk. We can dare to love, too. Nothing can threaten our sense of value. Nothing can undermine our confidence. Nothing can take God's love away. We can be *real*. We can help others become *real*, too: ". . . once you are Real you can't be ugly, except to people who don't understand."

There were times when giving and loving brought pain,
And I promised I would never let it happen again!
But I found out that loving was well worth the risk,
And that even in losing, you win.

I'm going to live the way He wants me to live.
I'm going to give until there's just no more to give.
I'm going to love, love 'til there's just no more love—
I could never, never outlove the Lord!

He showed us that only through dying we live,
And He gave 'til it seemed there was no more to give.
He loved when loving brought heartache and loss.
He forgave from an old rugged Cross.

I'm going to live the way He wants me to live.
I'm going to give until there's just no more to give.
I'm going to love, love 'til there's just no more love—
I COULD NEVER, NEVER OUTLOVE THE LORD!

VI

Because He Lives . . .

*death dies, life wins, and there
is eternity in every moment.*

Because He Lives

Nothing is so central to the Good News of Abundant Life in Jesus Christ as the Resurrection. Without it there is no Good News, for the death of Jesus would have confirmed, not reversed, the cycle of death in humanity. Evil would once more have triumphed. The death factor that had been innate in humanity would have ridden in victory to the funeral of God's ultimate gift of Himself. Had there been no Resurrection, the death on the cross would have been the death of LIFE.

In the physical world, when a baby is born he begins the lifelong process of dying. It's a one-way street. There is no choice. He is born to die. As Reuben Welch puts it, the mortality rate is 100 percent. The cells and organs of the human body begin their aging process right at birth, and the death factor will sooner or later make its final claim. The physical body, though miraculously made, has no eternity in it. It is born to die.

Now this inevitable death factor was set in motion by the first act of willful disobedience in the Garden of Eden. God did not originally intend that there should be such a thing as death and decay. Death was not an intention. It was a result. Had there been no sin, there would have been no death. Had there been no disobedience, there would have been no resulting pain. But with disobedience was born the death factor, and that death factor has ultimately laid claim to every person who has ever lived. It begins to make its claim the moment a physical child is born and it eats away at life until it has devoured the whole of it.

It was the creative energy of God's love that came to the rescue with redemption's plan. God Himself would "buy back" man's right to life by coming to earth as a man, living without sin, then choosing to die for the sins of all humanity. God's coming-to-earth-as-a-man was called Jesus, and—in Jesus—God was choosing *death* for no crime of His own, in order to make it possible for man to choose LIFE for no virtue of his own. It was a trade-off between Jesus and justice. Jesus paid everything; man paid nothing. Man had chosen disobedience, and with it came death, both physical and spiritual. Now it would be possible for man to reverse his direction. He could choose LIFE. Physical death would have to remain a part of human life on earth as a reminder of man's first tragic choice. But now man would be offered a new kind of life. Like the physical life, it would begin with a birth, but *this* life would not be subject to death. The death factor could not touch it. Decay would have no dominion in this new world. By accepting God's plan, people could be born into this new sphere and a whole new kind of life would begin. This was Abundant Life with eternity in it. There would be a new body, not seen with physical eyes. There would be new days and new food and new shelter and new values and new affections. And this New Life could start in the time space of the human existence, here and now. It would be a whole other world—a Kingdom, Jesus had called it—in the hearts of men.

So the angel and the manger and the miracles and flawless life and the crucifixion all stood with the women at the empty tomb that Easter morning.

"He is not here!"

"He is risen!"

"Behold, the place where he lay!"

To the women it was good news!

To the rest it was the culmination!

Life had conquered death!

All that Jesus had come to do had ended, not in death, as the physical laws would demand, but in LIFE! Death had been swallowing life since the Garden of Eden, but on this morning, it was death that had been swallowed up in victory! No wonder the women ran to tell the news!

Life was dancing on the grave of death itself! The vicious cycle of the death factor had been circumvented. Foiled! The headlines of the universe would forever publish the news: LIFE CONQUERS DEATH!—and poets would begin to shake their pens at death with lines like these:

> Death, be not proud, though some have called thee
> Mighty and dreadful, for thou art not so;
> For those whom thou think'st thou dost overthrow
> Die not, poor Death; nor yet canst thou kill me. . . .
> One short sleep past, we wake eternally,
> And Death shall be no more; Death, thou shalt die.
>
> JOHN DONNE

What a celebration! The work that had been finished on the cross had bought back LIFE! Death would have no more dominion. New birth was a reality!

Spring had come to the soul, the shackles of eternal winter had been broken, and men and women and children could once more be made truly alive!

Shout it in the streets!

Tell it to the children!

Sing it to the wrecked!

Share it with the hopeless!

Tack a sign on every altar:

ETERNITY STARTS HERE!

And as the women shared the glorious news with the disciples, the words they had heard Jesus say (that had seemed at times to be obscure) began to have marvelous meaning for their days. "The kingdom of God is within you," He had said. "The kingdom of God cometh not with observation." (*See* Luke 17:20). "My kingdom is not of this world," He had told Pilate.

And He had spoken so often about life. "Life doesn't have to do with the things you own," He had told them. "I am the resurrection, and the life: he that believeth in me, though he were dead, yet shall he live. And whosoever liveth and believeth in me shall never die . . ." He had told Martha (John 11:25, 26).

The woman of Samaria had shared then how He had offered her *living water.* "The water I shall give shall be a well of water springing up into everlasting life!" (*see* John 4:14).

"He is risen!—He is alive!"

With that announcement came new meaning for His words, new definition for the days that they had spent with Him. Resurrection was going to mean more than an empty tomb. It was going to be the dimension which the New Life would have in this new world, not only somewhere far out in the future, but now as well. Eternity was moving in—eternity in their hearts.

How fitting for the angel to have asked, "Why seek ye the living among the dead? He is not *here!*" Life is out of place in a sepulchre. Eternity is not at home in a grave. *You can't bury life!* Perhaps, too, the angel was predicting that those who would choose to be possessed by the Resurrection would never be at home in the places of the dead. Perhaps he was intimating that although they walked this physical world where death and decay still held sway, they would never again belong; they would be only pilgrims passing through the graveyard of earth. Their hearts would never set up permanent residence here, for they would be on their way to the "homeland of the living."

Each time the disciples saw their Master—just outside

the sepulchre, on the road to Emmaus, behind the closed doors, on the seashore at dawn, and along with five hundred other believers—they knew that it was all true: LIFE had won! Jesus was alive, alive in a new and spectacular way. A way that knew no limits, no boundaries, no end. It was a life that turned the tables on all earthly sense of values. Beside it, what they had once thought was reality now looked plastic, poor and shoddy by comparison. The things that had once seemed so important to them now faded and disappeared from view. What they had called "life," they now could see, had been only creeping death. *This* was LIFE. *This* was reality.

This new reality—the Real Thing—would have to be kept alive by new and different food. It would find its shelter only in the hearts of men and women. It would come to possess them not by conquering but by submission. Suddenly, His New Life in them was all that mattered. The world around them was shaky and uncertain. No matter. His Word was sure. The economy around then was poor. No matter. This Abundant Life was fed lavishly from the boundless resources of His Kingdom. Their future in this world was precarious. This New Life was eternal.

No wonder He had told them again and again about losing to win, giving it all up to gain everything! "Seek ye first the kingdom," He'd told them, "and *all things* will be added unto you!

"Don't lay up treasures here," He had said. "The things of this world are still subject to decay. Count your wealth by the treasures you possess that are not subject to death!"

No wonder the sword could not silence these new creatures in Christ Jesus! No wonder the lions could not devour their joy, the dungeons could not entomb their excitement, the assassins could not still their secret, and the catacombs only echoed their message: *Jesus is alive, and because He lives we too shall live!*

And still today, nearly 2,000 years later, the citizens of this new country, those "born of the Spirit," are echoing the song of life and are spreading the news of the Resurrection. LIFE is the winner!

For those of us who have been possessed by the New Life factor, it has brought meaning and courage and a whole new set of values to our days.

It gives us the energy to function—joyfully!—in a world filled with depressing news and tragic pessimism. It gives us the courage to take the risk of meaningful relationships, to begin marriages, and to rear children. The joy of being possessed by this New Life drives us to walk boldly among the dying, bringing the news of the Resurrection.

Now, may I reduce all this to simple and personal terms and tell you what it means in my life? I am a wife and a mother. It was in the middle of the upheaval in the sixties that we were expecting our third baby. The drug culture was in full swing, existential thought had obviously saturated every area of our American thought, the cities were seething with racial tension, and the God-is-dead pronouncement had giggled its way all through our educational system. On the personal front, Bill and I were going through one of the most difficult times in our lives. Bill had been discouraged and physically exhausted by a bout with mononucleosis, and in that weakened condition had little reserve to fight the psychological battle brought on by some external family problems. Someone whom we had cared about a great deal had hurled some accusations at us and at the Fellowship of Believers and at the whole idea of the existence of God.

It was on New Year's Eve that I sat alone in the darkness and quiet of our living room, thinking about the world and our country and Bill's discouragement and the family problems—and about our baby yet unborn. *Who in their right mind would bring a child into a world like this?* I thought. *The world is so evil. Influences beyond our con-*

trol are so strong. What will happen to this child?

I can't quite explain what happened at that moment, but suddenly I felt released from it all. Have you ever seen a little girl who is shaking with fear or hysterical with apprehension because she is lost? Have you seen the child's father take her face in both his hands and gently, yet firmly, turn her face toward his until their eyes meet and the child becomes conscious that her daddy is there? That is the nearest I can come to telling you how I felt. The panic that had begun to build inside was gently dispelled by a reassuring presence that engulfed my life and drew my attention.

Gradually, the fear left and the joy began to return. I knew I could have that baby and face the future with optimism and trust. I knew that God knew our motives, and He knew our hopes and our concern for the person who had brought us heartache. I knew that the unlimited strength and power of the Holy Spirit was at our disposal in this time of physical and spiritual and emotional exhaustion. It was the Resurrection affirming itself in our lives once again. It was LIFE conquering death in the regularity of my day.

It has happened many times in different ways. LIFE conquering death. People often ask, "How can you be so happy?" and it's hard to explain. It doesn't seem to have anything to do with the circumstances of life in which we find ourselves. The deep joy keeps bubbling up and taking precedent over all the frightening, depressing human circumstances. When the Resurrection principle comes to possess us, death has no more dominion. There is no earthly power that can kill LIFE!

One day in the late fall, we had some men come to pave the parking lot behind our office. They brought load after load of coarse rocks, pea gravel, and sand. They brought huge heavy rollers and smashed all of that down. Again and again they rolled it. Finally came the steaming truckloads of molten asphalt to be poured atop the gravel, then rolled again and again until it was smooth and hard and "permanent."

Very early the next spring, Bill's dad came into the office one morning, and stood around on first one foot then the other, grinning as he does when there's something special on his mind. "Come out here," he finally said to Bill and me. We followed him out the back door onto the shining new pavement. Right in the middle of it he stopped and pointed, "Look, there." Up through the sand, up through the gravel, up through the rocks, up from the darkness and through the thick layer of asphalt had pushed a green shoot. It wasn't tough; it wasn't sharp, it wasn't strong. Any child could have plucked it up with nearly no effort at all. *But it was alive!* And there it stood, bright green in the sunlight, boasting to the world of its photosynthetic miracle: *life wins!*

There wasn't much to say. We just smiled our message of reassurance at each other; but I couldn't help thinking of the song we had just written after our own personal bout with darkness:

> God sent His Son; they called Him Jesus.
> He came to love, heal and forgive.
> He bled and died to buy my pardon;
> An empty grave is there to prove
>   MY SAVIOR LIVES.
>
> How sweet to hold our newborn baby,
> And feel the pride and joy he gives;
> But greater still the calm assurance:
> Our child can face uncertain days
>   BECAUSE HE LIVES.
>
> Because He lives
>   I can face tomorrow!
> Because He lives
>   All fear is gone!

Because I know
    He holds the future,
And life is worth the living
    JUST BECAUSE HE LIVES!

There are still times when the cares of this world dis-tract us and "cause the heart to tremble," but time after time the power of Abundant Life pulls our attention back to the Real Things, the things with eternity in them, and we sing with the writer: "Thou hast put eternity in our hearts!"

There are some lovely lines written by a poet long since graduated from this earth to the place where life has no distractions. Because his words were true, they are still alive:

A Psalm of Life

Tell me not, in mournful numbers,
    Life is but an empty dream!
And the soul is dead that slumbers,
    And things are not what they seem.

Life is real! Life is earnest!
    And the grave is not its goal;
Dust thou art, to dust returnest
    Was not spoken of the soul.
        HENRY WADSWORTH LONGFELLOW

And then one day I'll cross that River;
I'll fight life's final war with pain.
And then as death gives way to victory,
I'll see the lights of glory,
    and I'll know He reigns.
BECAUSE HE LIVES!

Thank God for the Promise of Springtime

Winter this year in Indiana has been long and hard. The old-timers say they can't remember anything like it. The snows began in earnest soon after Christmas, although we had had flurries and some ground cover as early as Thanksgiving. When the big snows started, the children were delighted! They bundled into their snowsuits and raced for the hillside with their sleds. Bill and I went out, too, and helped them pack a sled trail clear to the fence. After they tired of sledding, they began to build a giant snow fort just outside the family-room window, taking turns with the block mold which Grandma had given them for Christmas. Next they shoveled the snow from the frozen creek and went ice-skating. They lapped up quarts of hot chocolate and warmed themselves at the crackling kitchen fire, then out they'd go again. They played with winter with that ardent passion of youngsters who have learned from experience that the days of the deep snow are very limited and must be made the most of while they last.

But this year the warming did not come. The snow stayed, and more was added to it. The mercury continued to drop—to zero, then down to unheard-of levels for central Indiana. At times it plummeted to as low as twenty-four degrees below zero, and with those temperatures came gale winds that pushed the wind-chill factor to seventy below. Gradually, our old friend winter became our dangerous enemy. People struggled to keep warm. The bitter cold and drifting snow closed the school for weeks on end, stranded and killed motorists, and threatened industry with fuel cutbacks to save the dwindling reserves for necessary home use. Grocery shelves began to empty because delivery trucks could not get through. There wasn't enough milk in our stores to meet the demands of all the babies and children. Water pipes in homes froze and broke; furnaces were overworked to keep up with the frigid temperatures. People without water or heat faced the terror of learning that repairmen were stranded and unable to help. The warm fire that Bill keeps burning for us in the kitchen became more than a cozy luxury. It was a necessity; and running out of wood was not just an inconvenience but a threat. Suddenly, tales of man's ancient struggle with the elements became stark reality.

Children could not be let out-of-doors because of the sure threat of instant frostbite. Animals froze to death or were cut off from food supplies. Helicopters searched the countryside for tops of fence posts in hopes of locating buried roadways, so that help could reach those caught without adequate supplies. One lovely new home only two miles out of town burned to the ground because the fire trucks were unable to reach it.

The gray days have stretched into weeks. The children have been out of school more than a month. But today the airports are cleared and the temperature has returned to normal for this time of year, so with the children we are on our way to an engagement in the West. The jet plane has just burrowed its way through the thick gray, then white, cloud cover, and we've just broken through to sunshine. Sunshine! Its brilliance is almost blinding to my unaccustomed eyes. It's been so long, I'd almost forgotten how bright a day can be. I guess somewhere in the back of my mind I knew that the sun would break through, come spring. But I had just not thought about it being there, somewhere above the clouds, all along—all through the dark winter. Somehow just this glimpse of it makes me know that I can go back to face the rest of winter with a better sense of perspective and joy. When I get back, I will have been reminded. The sun is still there! Even in winter, even in the midst of the storm, even when everything seems dead and dark, the sun is still there. Somewhere, up above the clouds, it still shines and warms and pulls at the life buried deep inside the brown branches and frozen earth. The sun is there! Spring will come! The clouds cannot stay forever.

And while the clouds are here I must remember that they can never extinguish the sun; they can only hide it for a while from my point of viewing. When I get home, I will remember and I will sing. When I see the snow drifts, I will think "roses"! When I see the "dead" brown twigs, I will think "foliage"! When I hear the wind, I will think "warm breezes." And when I see gray, I will think "blue skies" and "living things," for God has promised:

> While the earth remaineth, seedtime and harvest, and cold and heat, and summer and winter, and day and night shall not cease.
>
> Genesis 8:22

Thank God for the promise of Springtime!
Once again my heart will sing!
There's a brand new day a-dawning,
Thank God for the promise of Spring!

Though the earth seemed bleak and barren,
And the seeds lay brown and dead;
The promise of life throbbed within them,
And I knew Spring was just ahead.

Though the skies be gray above me,
And I can't see the light of day;

There's a ray breaking through the shadows,
And His smile can't be far away.

Thank God for the promise of Springtime!
Once again my heart will sing!
There's a brand new day a-dawning!
THANK GOD FOR THE PROMISE OF SPRING!

And when the hard times of life come, we will remember the "winter of '77." We will know that no matter how tragic the circumstances seem, no matter how long the spiritual drought, no matter how long or dark the days, the sun is sure to break through; the dawn will come. The warmth of His assurance will hold us in its embrace once again, and we will know that our God has been there all along. Hard times come to every man. Until the grip of this old world is forever broken by that final blast from Gabriel's trumpet, we will go on having seasons of winter here on earth. No man is exempt from heartache. But the night cannot last forever, and the darkest hour is just before the dawn. God has promised that "though weeping endures for the night, joy comes in the morning!" (*see* Psalms 30:5).

If you've knelt beside the rubble
    Of an aching, broken heart;
When the things you gave your life to
    Fell apart;
You're not the first to be acquainted
    With sorrow, grief or pain;
But the Master promised sunshine after rain.

Hold on, my child!
    Joy comes in the morning!
Weeping only lasts for the night.
Hold on, my child!

> *Joy comes in the morning!*
> The darkest hour means dawn is just in sight!
>
> To invest your seed of trust in God
>   In mountains you can't move,
> You have risked your life on things
>   You cannot prove;
> But to give the things you cannot keep
>   For what you cannot lose,
> Is the way to find the JOY God has for you.

Even So, Lord Jesus, Come

There's a golden time of evening, just before children sleep, when little people open up their hearts and invite you to come in. They never let you stay long, only long enough to look around. It is a foolish parent who would turn down such a special invitation, for the treasures that can be glimpsed at these fleeting and limited moments are indeed rare.

"Mother," Amy said to me one evening, after I had accepted such an invitation and had snuggled in beside her long enough to give her the time it takes to fumble open the door-latch of her heart, "Mother, when we die — [*slowly, thoughtfully*]—when we die, do we go to heaven?—or does heaven come to us?"

I waited, trying to judge by inadequate weights and measures the potential value of this treasure about to be placed in my hands. "I mean, Mommy, do you believe in chariots?"

"The Bible speaks of chariots, honey," I began carefully.

"There have been people who have said they saw them in visions. I don't know if they were actual chariots or whether people just chose that word to explain something we have no word to express. Why do you ask?"

"Well, what I really want to know is: Does something take us to heaven, or does heaven come to us?" She paused a moment, thinking. . . . "It seems to me that being here holds heaven back, but when we die, heaven can just come on in."

Wow! The immensity of the room she'd opened up to me almost took my breath away. There was little I could say. I mumbled something simple like, "You may be right, babe; you may be right," and kissed her sleepy eyes. I could feel the door closing gently behind her as she floated off into the world of dreams, but the wonder of the truth she'd let me glimpse remained indelibly imprinted in my mind.

Her insight was so clear, so simple. Of course! It is the limitations of our humanness that shackle us to this time-world, that keeps "heaven" pushed back and away. *But when we die, heaven can just come on in.*

As Amy slept peacefully, I began my own pilgrimage down the path of insight on which she had started me. Yes, Amy. When we come to Jesus, it must be then that we begin to let heaven in. The more we can let go of the earth in us, the more of heaven can come in. It's a lifelong process of gradually submitting areas of our lives so that heaven can move into them. But being tied to this earth by our physical bodies will always hold heaven back in its fullness. We aren't equipped to take it in. We couldn't contain the glory. But when death comes, it crumbles the containers of earth—these physical vessels—and lets heaven flood in. Eternity that has begun in our hearts can then completely possess us!

What a beautiful, simple way to clear up the mystery of "heaven"! Once again I stood in awe of the wisdom of a child. I had heard great discussions and read impressively difficult theological theories about heaven, but here was the whole picture—so simple, so obvious. *Out of the mouth of babes* . . . (Psalms 8:2). *God has chosen the wisdom of the simple to confound the wise* (*see* 1 Corinthians 1:27). It wasn't that this life is *here,* and heaven was *out there* somewhere beyond the blue. Heaven was all around, just waiting for us to let it in. I thought of all those wonderful times when the Holy Spirit had been so near and special, those times when for a few moments we had glimpsed and held a bit of heaven. How filling and satisfying were those tasty morsels, and yet how hungry and thirsty they made us for more, more, more! How often we have shared the passion of the Psalmist who wrote: "As the hart panteth after the water brooks, so panteth my soul after thee, O God. My soul thirsteth for God, for the living God" (Psalms 42:1, 2).

How often after a long spiritual drought, when the shackles of earth had caused us to live by blind and stubborn faith, we have prayed for those rich, sweet, refreshing times of knowing that heaven is still there, waiting on the outskirts of this time-world to pour in and possess us. How thankful we have been that the Comforter has come to lift the veil that holds heaven back and let in enough of it to fill the spaces we have hollowed out with the shovels of our commitment. So often we have prayed:

> Come, Holy Spirit, I need Thee!
> Come, Sweet Spirit, I pray!
> Come, in Thy strength and Thy power;
> Come in Thy own gentle way.
>
> Come, like a spring in the desert,
> Come, to the withered of soul;
> O let Thy sweet, healing power
> Touch me and make me whole.

Come, as a wisdom to children,
Come, as new sight to the blind,
Come, Lord, as strength to my weakness;
Take me: soul, body, and mind.

Come, as a rest to the weary,
Come, as a balm for the sore;
Come, as a dew to my dryness,
Fill me with joy evermore.

It is difficult to explain to those who have never tasted of eternity, the hunger and thirst that drives us to the cool springs and the manna of the Spirit. I know it wasn't always easy for me to understand the excitement which Christians felt about meeting together to feast on the Word or share their songs of praise and joy. But now I know, because I've tasted it for myself, that the greatest riches this world can boast can never compare to even one limited morsel of the good things of the Lord.

You're right, Amy. We've plugged into eternity, and heaven is all around us, just waiting to come on in. One day we will be completely possessed by the reality to which we have given ourselves in faith here.

I think I know how you happened to make your discovery. It was when Grandpa died. How you had loved him: the way he would carry you and Benjy around on his back, pretending he was a bucking bronco and you were wild desperadoes—the way he would sit and read to you and share his bedtime bowl of cornflakes—the way he'd take you for walks by the brook and point out cracks in the duck eggs that were just beginning to pip.

You were with us that weekend in Kansas City, but we didn't tell you until we were nearly home, that next morning on the plane, why we had been called back. I worried about telling you. I was afraid you wouldn't understand, since you were only five. But your daddy and I decided that, since death was a part of life, we should just be as honest and simple as we could in telling you. We did not shield you, only prepared you as best we could to help fill, with extra love and presence, the vacuum Grandpa's absence would make for Grandma.

It was at the funeral home that I knew you understood, maybe better than we did. You wanted to touch Grandpa's hand. At first, I almost said no, but quickly thought better of it. As you touched his hand you turned your little face to me. It was filled with comprehension. "Grandpa isn't here, is he?" you asked. "His old body that gave him so much trouble is here, but Grandpa's not here, is he?"

"No dear," I answered as best I could. "That part of Grandpa that twinkled and chuckled and loved and felt and reached out to hold you—that part is more alive than ever—with Jesus. But his old body with the old heart that gave him so much trouble is still here. We'll bury it with his suit and his shoes and the other things he used to wear. He won't mind. He won't need them anymore."

Since then you have talked of him often, usually in the present tense. You have helped us all to understand by your simple faith that Grandpa is more alive now than he's ever been, because he's no longer limited by the restrictions his body and his humanity used to place on him. He can love—perfectly. He can *be*—freely. He can fully satisfy his thirst to learn that was always hampered by the limited opportunities this life afforded him. Any investment he made—in time, in effort, in affection, in the things that have eternity in them—only gave him a head start on heaven. Any spiritual growth and any learning and wisdom he gained while he was here only widened his capacity to enjoy heaven when it finally "came on in."

Amy, when I was your age, Grandpa was a preacher. After he died we found a folder he had left of special things he wanted to say to you and to all of us. One of the things in the folder was a sermon he had preached on a favorite verse of his from the Bible. I've heard him preach on it many times. It goes like this:

> ... I know whom I have believed, and am persuaded that he is able to keep that which I have committed unto him against that day.
>
> Hold tightly to the pattern of truth I taught you, especially concerning the faith and love Christ Jesus offers you. Guard well the splendid, God-given ability you received as a gift from the Holy Spirit who lives within you.
>
> I say this because I won't be around to help you very much longer. My time has almost run out. Very soon I will be on my way to heaven. I have fought long and hard for my Lord, and through it all I have kept true to him. And now the time has come for me to stop fighting and rest. In heaven a crown is waiting for me which the Lord, the righteous Judge, will give me on that great day of his return. And not just to me, but to all those whose lives show that they are eagerly looking forward to his coming back again.

2 Timothy 1:12

2 Timothy 1:13, 14 LB

2 Timothy 4:6–8 LB

Isn't that special, Amy? You see, when we begin our walk with the Lord, life begins there. Nothing, not even death, can interrupt it. When we are born in Jesus, death can't stop our lives; it can only make them better. The other day I came to visit your school. Remember? I brought chocolate-chip cookies and a book to read to your class and had such a happy time with you and your friends. At the beginning of the day, your teacher called the roll. She said, "Mindy," and Mindy said, "Present."

"Tommy."

"Present."

"Amy."

"Present."

Some children didn't answer. They couldn't say, "Absent," could they? Well, the Bible says the death of a Christian is like that. We're alive whether we're at home or at school. We just can't be present both places at once.

When Daddy and I take you with us on trips, your teacher says it's fine, because you learn so much more than you would at school. At school you study places in a book. Sometimes there are pictures of those places for you to look at, but your teacher says that's not as good as really *going* there, seeing those places for yourself, eating the food, hearing the way the people talk, feeling the climate. She's glad for you to go, because she knows how much you're learning. But on those days when she calls the roll and all the children say, "Present," you don't answer when she comes to your name. You can't. You're absent. Absent from school. But present with Daddy and me in a new place.

The Bible says heaven is like that. We're alive both here and there if we belong to Jesus, but we're *more* alive there because it's the *real* side of life, not just a story of life or a picture of life, as we have to sometimes settle for here.

"To be absent from the body is to be present with the Lord," the Bible says (*see* 2 Corinthians 5:8).

Present here. Absent there. Absent here. Present there.

But really, you said it best. Being here holds heaven back, but when we die, heaven can just come on in—fully, completely, totally. I love you for helping me see that beautiful thought. You, there, floating in your secret world of slumber. Thank you for being a child, for giving us the glimpses only a child can give of things eternal. I think Wordsworth was right: "The child *is* father of the man." Children are so "lately come from God."

> When my eyes shall span that river,
> When I gaze into the vast unknown,
> May I say with calm assurance,
> "Even so, Lord Jesus, come."
>
> Even so, Lord Jesus, come,
> My heart doth long for Thee!
> Though I've failed and betrayed Thy trust,
> Even so, Lord Jesus, come.

Come on in, Lord Jesus, heaven, eternity. Come in a little at a time, as I hollow out spaces by obedience and trust. Or come in totally, as I am freed by death to be fully engulfed by the wonders of glory. I want all there is available to me—now—and ever.

We Have This Moment

Focus. That is the problem. Living amidst the distractions of the terminal and tinsel of this world, the challenge is to keep zeroing in on those things that are eternal and to devote our time and energies to those things that feed the part of us that will live forever. We must be able to recognize the eternity in a moment, and to nurture those things that are life-giving, if we are to *be* LIFE and to *bring* LIFE to an ailing world.

The Word of God says that we must "fix our minds on

things above, not on things of the world" (*see* Colossians
3:2). If we take Jesus as our example, that verse does not
suggest that we walk around in some kind of ethereal
trance with our heads in the clouds, blanking out the pain
and joys of our surroundings. Instead (we could rephrase
it this way): "Think *'forever.'*" Every day is filled with
choices and value judgments about where and how to
spend our time and energies. In deciding which things are
worth that investment, think *forever*. Bill likes to say it
like this: "Sir, when you're sixty-five or seventy and
you look back on today, make sure you'll say about the
choice you're about to make, 'Now, *that* was really worth
it!' "

Bill and I wrote a song one time called "That's Worth
Everything." Before writing it, we actually sat down with
pencil and paper to make a list of those things in our lives
that were "worth everything." Our list was not very long:

> To know when tiny feet walk in the path
>   That I have left behind,
> That they will make their way to Jesus,
>   Contentment there to find.
> And just to know down deep within my heart
>   That I have wronged no man,
> To fit my Master's plan,
>   That's worth everything.
>
> Just to know the future's His forever,
>   Just to feel the freedom of a child;
> Just to know the past is gone
>   And sunshine's here to stay,
> And He is Lord of all—
>   Oh, that's worth everything.

The next problem is to ask ourselves whether the way we actually spend our time confirms the priorities of our list. Do our moments prove that we are learning to think *"forever"?* That is a harder question. We can throw off the burden of responsibility for making a statement to the world on grounds of money or influence or prestige or social opportunity. But time is the great leveler.

When it's all said and done, we all have basically the same raw material with which to work in this life, and that raw material is time. We may be poverty-stricken—or financially secure. We may be physically attractive—or something less than Raquel Welch or Robert Redford. We may function in a stratum of society that is privileged and sophisticated—or our names may never appear on anybody's "social register." But all of us have equal time: twenty-four hours a day. It is with this raw material that we make the statement of our lives. Moments. Life is made up of them.

We tend to think of a moment as something incidental or unimportant, but the priorities of moments, compiled, make up the priorities of our lives. The value judgments of moments, averaged out, comprise our value systems. The statements we make with our moments confirm or deny the statements we make with our mouths.

Underestimating the value of a moment to life is like saying that the atom is not important to our earth in comparison with the importance of grand and giant buildings, factories, and roadways. Disrespect for the qualities and potential of the atom would be very foolish indeed, if we claim to value our physical world. The simple fact that the atom is microscopic does not diminish its potential for stability or destruction.

In a single moment, there is potential to salvage or destroy an entire lifetime, and it is with the priceless resource of moments that we either misuse or bring Real Life to those who share those moments with us. There is the potential for eternity in every moment, if it is used to feed that part of us or of those around us that will live forever—the spirit.

It is not so much the big things that kill or nurture the spirit; it is the "little things." Funny. It seems that we have the terms turned around. It's nearly always the little moments that are the giant milestones of life. I recall just now a little rhyme from "The Spring And The Fall" by Edna St. Vincent Millay that says:

> 'Twas not love's going hurt my days,
> But that it went in little ways.

The little things seem to be the carriers for the food of the Spirit. The "bread of life we just can't live without" is nearly always fed to us in little bites. How many marriages could be kept alive if husbands could realize that sometimes a wife needs a rose more than she needs a loaf of bread or a quart of milk? How many husbands would stay communicative and productive if a wife could perceive that once in a while his need for her to drop everything, grab some bologna sandwiches, and go to a ball game or on a fishing trip (and really enjoy it!) is greater than his need for a spotless house or a gourmet dinner? How many children could be salvaged if parents could understand that kids don't need toys and bicycles nearly so much as they need an hour of unpreoccupied attention in which they are openly and unashamedly enjoyed and appreciated as persons by the two people whose opinions they most value? What if parents together could view parenthood as more than braces and hamburgers, baseball mitts and new saddle shoes?

What would happen if we who share the same houses and neighborhoods and churches could hear the things that are *not* being said as clearly as we hear what is being shouted? What if we all were to make it a point of hearing

with our hearts, to recognize silence as a statement, to
give what we most need, and to share with others that for
which we most long ourselves?

As we look back over our lives, it is often the incidental
moments, the things *we almost missed* that molded the
direction and contents of our days. I remember, for instance, the moment when I first became aware that the
tables had turned on my relationship with my parents,
when I first realized that I needed to take some responsibilities for putting good things into their days, and for
understanding them, instead of always expecting to be
understood. It happened this way:

> If everything special and warm and happy in my
> formative years could have been consolidated into one
> word, that word would have been CHRISTMAS. So, by
> the time the building blocks of my days had piled
> themselves into something as formidable as late adoles-
> cence, Christmas had a lot to live up to.
>
> Christmas, by then, meant fireplaces and the bustle
> of a big, excited family, complete with aunts, uncles,
> and cousins. It meant great smells from the kitchen:
> homemade bread, cranberries bubbling on the stove,
> pumpkin pies, and turkey. It meant Grandma's cheery
> voice, racing to be the first to holler, "Christmas Gift!"
> as we came in the door. It meant real cedar Christmas
> trees, handmade foil ornaments, and lots of secrets. It
> meant enfolding in the arms of our great family the
> lonely or forsaken of our village who had no place to
> go. It meant all the good and lovely things we said
> about Christmas being in your heart and the joy being
> in the giving.
>
> Then came that other year.
>
> There were many things that conspired, as it were,
> to bring me to the laboratory situation in which I
> would test all my so glibly accepted theories. Grandma

was gone, leaving in my heart a vacuum that wouldn't go away. My sister had married by then and had the responsibility of sharing her holidays with her husband's people. The other relatives were far away. After a lifetime of serving in the ministry, Daddy had that year felt directed to resign his flock with no other pastures in mind and "wait on the Lord." Since I was away at college, just beginning my first year, I wasn't there when he and Mother moved from the parsonage to the tiny cottage at the lake that a concerned businessman had helped them build. Nor was I prepared that winter day for the deserted barrenness that can only be found in resort areas built solely for summertime fun.

There was no fireplace. There was no bustle of a big, excited family. Gone was the sense of tradition and history that only the aged can provide, and gone was the thrill of the immediate future that comes with the breathless anticipation of children.

The dinner was going to be small, just for the three of us, and there just wasn't any *ring* in the brave attempt that Mother made at shouting, "Christmas Gift!" as I came in the door. Daddy suggested that, because I'd always loved doing it, he and I should go to the woods to cut our own tree. I knew that now, of all times, I could not let my disappointment show, so I put on my boots and my cheeriest face and off through the knee-deep snow we trudged into the Michigan woods. My heart was heavy, and I knew Mother was back at the stove, fighting back the tears —for all that was not there.

There was loveliness as the forest lay blanketed in its heavy comforter to wrap around the chill in my heart. Daddy whistled as he chopped the small cedar tree. (He always whistled when there was something bothering him.) As the simple tuneless melody cut through the frozen air, I got a hint of the silent burdens adults carry, and for the first time felt myself on the brink of becoming one. As I picked up my end of the scraggly, disappointingly small cedar, I also picked up my end of grown-up responsibility, and I felt the times shift. I was no longer a child to be sheltered and cared for and entertained. My folks had put good stuff in me. Now as I trudged back through the snow, watching the back of my father's head, his breath making smoke signals in the cold morning air, the weary curve of his shoulders, I vowed to put some good stuff back into their lives.

The day was somehow different after that. We sat around our little table, stringing cranberries and making foil cutouts. But it was not this time the activity of a child, but more like a ceremonial tribute to the childhood I somehow could never again afford and to the people who had filled it with such wealth and beauty.*

That was a moment. The commitment and adjustment that this moment has demanded since—of Bill and me and of my parents—has been at times difficult and at times glorious. But because of the fleeting moment, God has brought some things of eternal value into all of our lives. Several years later, while serving in a pastorate in Michigan, my father suffered a coronary, which, because of the pressures of the ministry, forced him into an early retirement. Our writing and publishing were getting to the place where we needed some extra help, so we asked them to move to Indiana to help us with orders and with our growing family. It was not easy for my father to leave a vocation he loved. It was not easy for him to work for his son-in-law, and it was not always easy for Bill to know how to relate to his father-in-law as both a close family

*"My Most Memorable Christmas." First appeared in *Moody Monthly,* October, 1975. Copyright 1975, Moody Bible Institute of Chicago. Used by permission.

member and as an employee. We had to learn together. My parents had a hard time at first, letting us help them financially, when they had spent their lives being responsible for me. I had to learn to be specific about what I needed Mother to do for me in helping with the children, when at the same time I was still her daughter and wanted to be obedient and respectful to her wishes and wisdom.

But because of the commitments that we all shared, to think "forever," to find eternity in the moments, God was able to bring beauty into our lives through some difficult days and make us all richer for it. When my father passed away several years later, Bill and I felt glad that we had done some growing together with him. Together we had hollowed out some capacity for eternity and widened our reservoirs for the "water of life." In a way we feel a part of the joy he is now experiencing, because of the eternity we shared in the moments we had together here. Perhaps the day will come when we have more invested in "forever" than we have invested here. The scales will tip and we'll be anxious to leave the confines of time and space.

In the meantime, we are learning to notice, to focus our attention on the things of real value, to think "forever." We're learning to choose *home* over house, *learning* over education, *growth* over status, *joy* over thrills, *treasures* over money, *total healing* over physical and spiritual analgesia, *making moments* over spending time. We're beginning to see that there is an overall tone to the routine of our days that is the spirit of our testimony, and that it is with our moments that we say what we really believe.

I remember that when I was in high school there was a popular song entitled "Memories Are Made of This." I like that title, especially the first part: "Memories Are Made," to which I'd like to add: ". . . on Purpose." We have to choose to make memories. If we want our children to treasure the philosophy of their home, we must create an atmosphere of joy and warmth to surround the statement we make. If we want to look back over a life and a marriage that was fulfilling and enriching, we must choose to put good things into the moments we spend together now. Good lives and good homes and good marriages and good relationships don't "just happen." They're made—on purpose.

We hear a lot these days about the "now." Mostly the "now" philosophy means doing one's own thing because *now* is all there is. It suggests that man is an end in himself (the cosmic accident) and that anything that gives him comfort or pleasure or a temporary sense of fulfillment is the thing to do. This "now" philosophy says we may do anything we please so long as it does not hurt anyone else, and even then, the benefit of the moment may justify the injury to another.

But with Resurrection Living, the life that follows the birth of His Spirit in us makes us recognize that "no man liveth unto himself," that there is no choice that does not affect others, and that every moment is pregnant with potential for eternity. The " 'now generation' of the Spirit" puts a value on the present moment, not because it's all there is, but because it has *forever* in it.

This doesn't necessarily mean feverishly trying to spend time doing "religious" or "churchy" things. It does mean investing our very lives in the things that bring content and meaning to the mundane minutes. It means being sensitized by the Savior. The result of the New Birth and the New Life of the Spirit is *not* becoming so "elevated" that we're blind to the evil around us, so "good" that we walk on and over people to get to our heavenly home, and so "holy" that we're scared to death we're going to be contaminated if we touch those infected by sin's diseases. On the contrary, the touch of the Master makes us *see*. When Jesus touched the blind man, scales fell from his eyes, and when He touches us, scales fall from our eyes, too. We see beauties we didn't know existed. We come alive in the world of the Spirit, the *real* world, and we see the hurts and pain, too, caused by the infection of evil and the façade of the temporary. It is that seeing which demands our energies and our moments.

If we are the Body of Christ, we are the instruments of healing; we are Jesus to the world. We are the love and the warmth and the sunshine of His presence. Sensitized by His Spirit we begin to see and listen and touch. We begin to weigh the moments for the eternity in them. Perhaps this is what the Psalmist meant when he said, "So teach us to number our days, that we may apply our hearts unto wisdom" (Psalms 90:12). Wisdom—the ability to recognize the eternity in a moment. The habit of thinking "forever." In the middle of the noise of traffic and clatter and voices calling for our attention, Jesus calls us to focus on the eternal—*in this moment.* And the irony is that the opportunity to recognize the "forever" in a moment only lasts an instant. If we fail to touch it and see it, it is gone, forever. James said about our span of life here, ". . . . It is even a vapour, that appeareth for a little time, and then vanisheth away" (James 4:14). We cannot grasp or hoard these vanishing moments, we can only draw from them the eternal, and send them on ahead in the form of treasures that will not rust.

> Hold tight to the sound of the music of living,
> Happy songs from the laughter of children at play;
> Hold my hand as we run through the sweet fragrant
>   meadows,
> Making memories of what was today.
>
> Tiny sound that I hear is my little girl calling
> For mommy to hear just what she has to say;
> My little son running there down the hillside
> May never be quite like today.

Tender words, gentle touch, and a good cup of coffee,
And someone that loves me and wants me to stay;
Hold them near while they're here, and don't wait for
  tomorrow,
To look back and wish for today.

Take the blue of the sky and green of the forest,
The gold and the brown of the freshly mown hay.
Add the pale shades of spring, and the circus of autumn,
And weave you a lovely today.

For we have this moment to hold in our hands,
And to touch as it slips through our fingers like sand,
Yesterday's gone, and tomorrow may never come,
But we have this moment *today.*

Over the past several years, I have kept a diary. Doing so has taught me one thing: The giant traumas of life—that I thought we couldn't live through—have turned out with the perspective of time to be not so important, after all. And the incidental everyday things that I thought were barely worth recording have been the major threads on which are woven the whole fabric of life. Sometimes I have been able to recognize the specialness of a moment. Sometimes I have failed miserably. This morning I am looking back over some of those entries:

Entry:
Busy day. Lots of interruptions—people who needed help and someone to listen. Bill's on a diet. I've lost five pounds. With Mother and Daddy we took the children and neighbor kids to see a film about Alaska. I hope there will be "nature" left for them to teach their children about. Lyndon Johnson died this evening. His enemies will be his friends tomorrow. ***This was a moment. . . .***

Entry:

Little Suzanne was sick in the night. I kept her home today and she seems much better. The day did her good. She slept three hours, read books, and listened to records. This was our night to watch *The Waltons*. We all shared a grapefruit and snuggled. Bill is beautiful, and I love him. It's nice to love someone—easily. *This was a moment. . . .*

Entry:

Everything that could possibly go wrong in a concert went wrong tonight: rude ushers, loud overhead fans, huge impersonal building, poor lighting, bad sound problems, fire marshall moving people in the middle of the most serious moment, ushers passing out flyers during a quiet song—everything! In spite of it all, the Spirit of the Lord broke through. "He is the ruler yet." *This was a moment. . . .*

Entry:

After an exhausting weekend, Bill woke me at 6:00 A.M. to tell me that the basement was full of water! The new water softener we had put in was installed wrong and overflowed with *brine* all over the carpet and everything. Good thing he woke up at 5:00 instead of 8:00. J. M. is coming for lunch. Her father died and she needs some loving support. *This was a moment. . . .*

Entry:

Went out and walked in the woods—all of us—tonight after school. *So* lovely, the smells of autumn: nuts, berries, dry leaves, rich earth; the sights of autumn: the riot of color, the flicker of a blue jay in the golden beech, the glimmer of a brook peeping here and there through the cover of leaves; the sounds and feel of autumn: the laughter and shouts of excited children, the whisper of the

breeze that threatens to turn chill with the breath of
winter, the horses running wild into the cavern, a squirrel
frantically racing with the fleeting season. *This was a
moment. . . .*

Entry:
Had company. Some copy due. Working on learning
arrangements for new album. Bill is so impatient when I
can't get my part, and I feel so stupid. I react with tears
and giving up. Went to bed upset with each other and
silent. My stomach feels like it's been stirred with an egg-
beater. *This was a moment. . . .*

Entry:
"Benjy," I said, as I was reading him to sleep, "are you
going to grow up to be a good strong man who loves Jesus
and is kind and loving to people?" "Yes!" he said. "And I
just want you to know, that even when I'm grumpy, I'm
not gonna grow up grumpy!" *This was a moment. . . .*

Entry:
Amy was so dear tonight singing, "He made me 'pe-
cial." She is surely a confection from God's candy kitchen.
Stopped for a hamburger after the concert and met some
"Jesus kids." Their faces were radiant. We knew right
away they were Christians. I wonder if they knew right
away that we were? *This was a moment. . . .*

Entry:
After an already exhausting weekend we had to sing at
a college tonight. We did our best to "feed the multitude."
I think we knew how the disciples must have felt. So little
to feed so many. But we, as they, just give God the little
that we have, and trust that He can make it go around. I
have a feeling that, weak as we felt for those who came
hungry and expecting to be fed, there was enough to fill.
This was a moment. . . .

Entry:

Went out to have lunch with the kids today at school. Amy was so pleased. Suzanne came over and whispered, "Mommy, thank you for coming today." I love those little buggers—all little children for that matter. So glad we can have them to give us an excuse for being *ourselves*. *This was a moment. . . .*

Entry:

Suzanne is at a marvelous age. We went horseback riding today. The trails were lovely. I watched her bouncing along in front of me, her long, blond hair streaming down her back, catching the occasional glint of the sunbeams through the foliage. I found myself worrying about her posture; she's right at the age to start slumping. Then my mind shifted to the other kind of posture. Lord, help her to stand tall in this world before You. Protect her from those things that might cripple her spirit and stunt her growth in You. Help her to grow straight and fine and true in the stature that really matters. *This was a moment. . . .*

Entry: This Day—Seattle, Washington . . .

The clouds have settled like a necklace around the peak of Mt. Rainier. Patches of sunlight are shining across the ripples of Puget Sound. This will be our last trip of the spring season before the summer, and the children are anxious for us all to stay home.

We are anxious, too. We had to miss Suzanne's sixth-grade "commencement" last night, but we called home afterward. Both grandmas were there to go with her, and we sent her some flowers to wear on her new dress, but still. . . . So many of the decisions of life are not between the good and the bad, but between the best and the best of the best. Sometimes it isn't easy to know.

Bill is back from doing some business by phone to tell me it is time to get the plane to Spokane. He is all excited about the idea we worked on together yesterday for a new musical for children. It will demand a lot of time and work —probably this summer—but there is such a need for a way to make children aware of their infinite potential to *become*—in Jesus.

The wheels of commerce are turning in the city streets below; people are rushing to begin another Friday.

THIS IS A MOMENT. . . .